W9-BOO-462

Literary Landmarks
of New York

*The Book Lover's Guide to the Homes
and Haunts of World-Famous Writers*

Marc Connelly

Harpo Marx

George S. Kaufman

Robert Sherwood

Dorothy Parker

Robert Benchley

Harold Ross

Heywood Brou[n]

Edna Ferber

Alexander Woollcott

Franklin Pierce Adams

Literary Landmarks of New York

The Book Lover's Guide to the Homes and Haunts of World-Famous Writers

Bill Morgan

with photographs from the Museum of the City of New York

UNIVERSE • NEW YORK

Dedication

In memory of Ted Wilentz

First Published in the United States of America in 2003
by Universe Publishing
a Division of Rizzoli International Publications, Inc.
300 Park Avenue South
New York, NY 10010

Copyright © 2002 by Bill Morgan

All rights reserved. No portion of this book may be reproduced, stored in a retrieval system, or transmitted in any form or by any means, electric, mechanical, photocopying, recording, or otherwise, without prior consent of the publishers.

Interior Design by Don Wise
Design Assistant: Cara Moore
Cover Design: Paul Kepple and Jude Buffum @ Headcase Design
Cover Illustration by Mary Lynn Blasutta

2003 2004 2005 2006 2007 / 10 9 8 7 6 5 4 3 2 1

Printed in the United States

Library of Congress Catalog Control Number: 2002111511
ISBN: 0-7893-0854-1

Contents

Lower East Side and East Village

Chelsea

Gramercy Park and Murray Hill

Midtown

Preface

New York City is a city of wonders, a city where dreams become realities. And there are always new wonders and new dreams. I am New York born and New York bred. Still, it startled me to learn that my native city is the oldest in the country, notwithstanding Boston, Philadelphia, Charleston, and Williamsburg. Oldest in years, yes, but a city, to paraphrase Ezra Pound, that is forever "making it new"—a magnet for change, the very model of a modern metropolis. This is best exemplified by its legendary skyline, a marvelous assemblage of verticality packed into a small space. As late as 1960, *The Encyclopedia of New York City* reports, New York contained half of all the world's skyscrapers of fifty stories or more. The visual effect never fails to excite. It brings forth an emotional response that adds to the sense of the city as a place of splendors and thrills, of heights and depths, perils and romance.

If the architecture of a city expresses its physical nature, its literary landmarks speak to its mind and spirit. They are the evidence of the stories of society and the lives lived in that society. New York's literary landmarks range from the Thomas Paine house of revolutionary times to the black metropolis that Harlem became in the twenties; from the Jewish Rialto of the Lower East Side that hummed and vibrated with the vitality of an immigrant community at the turn of the century, to Greenwich Village, seeded in the Italian coffee shops and restaurants that became the gathering places of the artists and writers who charged the atmosphere with avant-garde creativity.

Our guide to this treasure trove is Bill Morgan, editor, writer, archivist, librarian, bibliographer. The idea for the book grew out of his scholarly interest and curiosity—a curiosity which led him to explore the sites with an archaeologist's eye for detail—and since he is also an artist, with the special vision of the painter's eye.

Ted Wilentz

Publisher, Corinth Books
Owner, Eighth Street Book Shop

Introduction

When I asked my friend, Ted Wilentz, to write the preface to this book, he said, "You know, you really should include a section of 'invisible presences' to commemorate landmarks now lost to the wrecking ball." Although the limitations of this book didn't allow space enough for such a list, his comments got me thinking about what we've lost from our literary heritage due to our thirst for redevelopment. Since preservationists had become organized after losing Penn Station and nearly losing Grand Central, I thought that these issues were resolved. Certainly now such important pieces of New York City would not be lost so easily!

How discouraging then to follow the plight of Edgar Allen Poe's house at 85 East 3rd Street. while writing this book. A community group challenged New York University in their attempt to tear down Poe's old house and replace it with a thirteen-story addition to their law school. It was the last remaining building in Manhattan to have once sheltered this greatest of American writers. It seemed impossible to believe that it was being torn down by one of the cultural institutions that would normally be attempting to preserve it. Even the judge who ruled in the case seemed shocked by their actions, yet powerless to prevent it. He stated in his ruling, "From a historical, cultural, and literary point of view, Poe House should stand. Unfortunately, not even academia will champion its preservation."

A book like this becomes a record of what literary landmarks are here now and should be appreciated while we still have them to enjoy. Being able to point to a house and say that Mark Twain lived here, or Dylan Thomas died here, or Jack Kerouac wrote *On the Road* here, is not a mere luxury in a city like New York; it is a necessity. It shows today's poets and writers that these people were human, that they lived the same kinds of lives that we live, and that they are cherished by the city in which they did live. If this book helps just one young child realize that Langston Hughes lived in his very own neighborhood and was at the same time one of the greatest writers of his generation, then it will be worth it. Maybe someday he will help protect that house from the wrecking ball.

Bill Morgan

Statue of Liberty

New York Harbor

The New Colossus.

Not like the brazen giant of Greek fame,
With conquering limbs astride from land to land;
Here at our sea-washed, sunset-gates shall stand
A mighty woman with a torch, whose flame
Is the imprisoned lightning, and her name
Mother of Exiles. From her beacon-hand
Glows world-wide welcome, her mild eyes command
The air-bridged harbor that twin-cities frame.

"Keep, ancient lands, your storied pomp!" cries she
With silent lips. "Give me your tired, your poor,
Your huddled masses yearning to breathe free,
The wretched refuse of your teeming shore,
Send these, the homeless, tempest-tost to me,
I lift my lamp beside the golden door!"

Emma Lazarus.

November 2nd 1883.

"The New Colossus" manuscript by Emma Lazarus

Perhaps the most famous poem written in New York City, for its most famous landmark, *The New Colossus* was **Emma Lazarus's** (1849–1887)

sonnet to honor the principles represented by the Statue of Liberty. The entire poem has been inscribed on a brass tablet at the base of the statue which can be visited via ferry from Battery Park. The poem was written in 1883 to help raise the funds needed to build the pedestal on which the statue stands. Frédéric-Auguste Bartholdi's statue was a gift from the people of France to the people of the United States. The only condition was that the American people were to erect the base,

View of the Statue of Liberty

and it took ten years of fund-raising and a major effort from Joseph Pulitzer's newspapers to do that. At the celebrated unveiling on October 28, 1886, Lazarus read her poem to some of the one million people gathered for the parade and speeches by President Grover Cleveland and other politicians. It wasn't until 1903 that the plaque with the poem was placed there. In the meantime, Lazarus had died in 1887, at the age of thirty-eight, only a year after the monument's dedication. She had lived in the Village on East 10th Street and a plaque at No. 18 commemorates her residence there.

Federal Hall National Memorial

Wall and Nassau Streets

The literary history of New York began with its newspapers. The earliest battle for freedom of the press in the colonies took place in New York City in the eighteenth century. Usually, the Federal Hall National Memorial is pointed out as the location for the inauguration of George Washington as the first President of the United States. It is indeed important for that reason, but a large part of the exhibition space within the building is devoted to the memory of newspaper editor **John Peter Zenger** (1697–1746), whose history is also closely linked to this site.

Zenger was a German immigrant who arrived in New York in 1710 and worked for several years as an apprentice to **William Bradford**, the pub-

First issue of the
New York Weekly Journal

lisher of the city's first newspaper, *The New York Gazette*. The *Gazette*'s editorial policies were tightly controlled by the colony's governor, William Cosby. In 1733, a group opposed to the Governor's Royalist policies and financially corrupt administration, asked Zenger to publish an opposition newspaper, which became the *New York Weekly Journal*. After only a year, the Governor took steps to have the newspaper shut down. In 1734, the Sheriff, whom Zenger had called "a monkey of the larger sort," confiscated copies of the *Weekly Journal* and symbolically burnt them in the street at the corner of Wall and Nassau, the site at the time of New York's City Hall. This did not stop Zenger from continuing the publication of the newspaper, and as a result he was arrested. He was imprisoned in City Hall for nine months before his case came to trial in August 1735.

Governor Cosby had Zenger's lawyers disbarred just before the trial. It looked bleak for the printer until his supporters surprised the court by recruiting eighty-year-old

Wall Street, circa 1918

Andrew Hamilton, the most famous lawyer of the day, to travel from Philadelphia to defend him. The prosecution charged that Zenger's publication was libelous. Hamilton defended Zenger, proving that the statements were true and therefore not libelous. The jury found John Peter Zenger not guilty, but he wasn't freed until his supporters could raise enough money to pay for his jail expenses for the previous year's incarceration. The case was the precedent for freedom of the press, guaranteed fifty years later in the Bill of Rights. It also gave rise to the expression "Philadelphia lawyer," meaning one with a sharp mind, skilled at the manipulation of subtle legalisms. Zenger was later appointed public printer for both New York and New Jersey, but died in financial straits.

The first public building on this site was the seventeenth-century Dutch Stadt Huys, replaced in 1701 by the colonial City Hall. That building was remodeled in 1788 and renamed Federal Hall in time for Washington's inauguration in 1789. The current building is the third public building erected on the site. It was built in 1842 as the U.S. Custom House and used in later years as the U.S. Sub-Treasury Building. It is one of the finest Greek Revival examples in the city and is considered the Parthenon of public buildings in New York City.

Trinity Churchyard Cemetery
Broadway and Wall Street

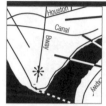

 T rinity Church's silhouette is familiar to most New Yorkers and stands proudly at the end of Wall Street. Although most people think that the current church is the original Revolutionary War–era structure, only the cemetery beside the church dates to the colonial period. The first church was built on this site in 1698 but destroyed by fire in 1776. Another building replaced it in 1790, but was demolished for structural reasons in 1839. The current Gothic Revival building, designed by Richard Upjohn, was dedicated in 1846. It is in the cemetery that we find an interesting literary tombstone.

Trinity Church offers a handy guide map which will help you find the marker—just inside the fence—on the north side of the church for **Charlotte Temple**'s grave. Marked by a name carved into the flat stone slab, Temple was supposedly born in 1756 and probably died around 1775, but in truth, no one knows if she really existed. The burial records for the church were destroyed in the great fire of 1776 and many of the graves are unmarked. In fact, Temple is the pseudonym of the person who may be interred here, Charlotte Stanley. Her tragic life became the subject of America's first romance novel, written in 1794 by America's first female novelist, **Susanna Haswell Rowson**. *Charlotte Temple: A Tale of Truth*, is the story of a young English girl who fell in love with a

Charlotte Stanley's tombstone

handsome British officer named Montresor, a name meaning "my treasure" in French. As he was being shipped off to New York to protect British interests against the colonists, Charlotte stowed away aboard his ship.

Upon their arrival in New York, she discovered that he was already married. Because she was pregnant, Montresor kept her out of sight until their child was born and then abandoned her in New York at the beginning of the turbulence leading to the Revolutionary War. Charlotte died wretched and lonely in the slums. The romantic tale was an early bestseller, printed in more than two hundred editions and unequaled in popularity until *Uncle Tom's Cabin* was published fifty years later. Though the brass marker identifying the grave of the real Charlotte Stanley had been missing for more than a hundred years, a workman, not knowing what her true name had been, carved her fictional name on this unmarked tombstone.

Trinity Church, Broadway and Wall Street

Horace Greeley Statue and Newspaper Row

City Hall Park, Park Row at the Brooklyn Bridge, near the corner of Chambers and Centre Streets

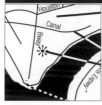

Standing in front of the Horace Greeley Statue next to City Hall, you are surrounded by several related literary sites. This was the center of journalism in nineteenth-century New York and the publishers of the daily and weekly newspapers, printers and typesetters, newsprint dealers, photographers, and lithographers filled the buildings which stood opposite City Hall on Park Row and Nassau Streets. Pre-eminent among these newspapermen was **Horace Greeley** (1811–1872), whose likeness, captured in the statue by John Quincy Adams Ward, was made directly from a cast of his death mask.

Horace Greeley came to New York City from New Hampshire at the age of twenty to begin his career as an editor. He soon became involved in politics, as well. He was the editor of leading Whig newspapers, *The Jeffersonian*, and *The Log Cabin*, and he founded New York's first daily Whig paper, *The New York Tribune*, in 1841. *The Tribune* was a financial success due to its wide distribution in the American West. Greeley used its pages for editorials espousing his views on important issues, such as the abolition of slavery and capital punishment, support for workers' and women's rights, and promotion of the Homestead Act of 1862, providing 160 acres of free land to homesteaders on the frontier. In a piece he wrote supporting the act, he used the lines that became most closely associated with him: "Go West, young man." Greeley acknowledged that the words were written by John Babsone Lane Soule for an article in the *Terre Haute Express* in 1851, but the quote is frequently attributed to

Greeley. Also published in Greeley's paper were Charles A. Dana, Charles Dickens, Margaret Fuller, William Dean Howells, Henry James, Karl Marx, Edgar Allan Poe, Carl Schurz, and Bayard Taylor. In 1872 Greeley ran for president but was defeated by Ulysses S. Grant.

It is appropriate that his statue be placed here, as the offices for *The New York Tribune* were across the street where the ramps to the Brooklyn Bridge are today. In fact, the statue was originally placed on private property in front of that building in 1890 and moved here in 1916. From the 1830s until the early twentieth century, all the New York newspapers had offices in this area, so that they could be close to City Hall events.

In 1893, there were nineteen daily newspapers in New York City and several foreign language papers as well. *The New York World* was published by **Joseph Pulitzer** and located just to the south of the Brooklyn

City Hall Park Looking East Toward Park Row, 1899

Bridge entrance. It was demolished, as was *The Tribune* building at 160 Nassau at Spruce Street. The *Associated Press* called 15 Park Row home (from 1899 to 1908 it was the world's tallest building); *The Recorder, The New York Daily News*, and both *The New York Press* and *The New York Observer* were at 21, 25, and 38 Park Row respectively. The original *New York Times* building is now part of Pace University at 41 Park Row; *The Sun, The Literary World*, and both *The Aurora* (where **Walt Whitman** worked for many years) and *The New York Union* were at 91, 109, and 111 Nassau Street respectively. *The Broadway Journal* was at the corner of Beekman and Nassau Street; *The Knickerbocker* and *The Mirror* were located at 139 and 148 Nassau Street. *New Yorker Staats-Zeitung*, the largest German-language newspaper in the city, was located where the Municipal Building is today on Centre Street opposite Chambers Street. *The New York American*, published by **William Randolph Hearst**, was a block away on William Street; and Currier & Ives, the printers, were located at 152 Nassau Street.

The importance of Newspaper Row faded as the newspapers began moving uptown, following the advance of the city's center. *The New York Herald,* later called *The Herald Tribune,* moved to Herald Square in 1894, and *The New York Times* moved to Times Square in 1904. Only a few vestiges of the old Newspaper Row remain today, presided over not only by the statue of Greeley, but also by a statue of **Benjamin Franklin,** across Park Row in Printing House Square. Perhaps best known as an inventor, statesman, and ambassador to France, Franklin was first and foremost a journalist, having founded the *Pennsylvania Gazette* in 1728. Franklin's statue was presented to the printers and pressmen of New York City by businessman Albert DeGroot as a tribute to their hard work and dedication to the profession of journalism. Horace Greeley presided at the unveiling ceremonies in 1872, the same year in which he died. After his death, Greeley's body lay in state in City Hall and was mourned by thousands.

Horace Greeley statue

21

Brooklyn Bridge

East River, Manhattan to Brooklyn

A wonder of the modern world when it opened in 1883, the Brooklyn Bridge has remained one of the most recognizable icons in the city and certainly its largest literary landmark. Numerous books have been written about the construction of the bridge from 1867 to 1883 and the changes prompted by its construction, (Vaudevillian Eddie Foy remarked "All that trouble just to get to Brooklyn!") One truly New York experience is to walk across the raised boardwalk in the middle of the bridge from Brooklyn to Manhattan for the exhilarating and memorable view. You'll see why the bridge has been the inspiration for hundreds of poems, thousands of paintings, and the scene of countless fictional events.

Even during construction, the bridge had a literary impact. **Frank Harris**, author of *My Life and Loves*, worked on building the bridge as a sixteen-year-old. But Harris lasted only a week or so, before he began suffering deafness from the "bends." The bends were caused by enormous pressure in the air locks of the caissons where workers remained for ten minutes at a time in order to build the bridge's great piers. The attrition rate of workers was staggering. Even the bridge's engineer, Washington Roebling, died from the effects of the bends.

Once completed, the Brooklyn Bridge became a symbol of progress to most Americans. **Walt Whitman** saw it as a link, not just between Brooklyn and New York, but between men of the past, present, and future: "The grand obelisk-like towers of the bridge, one on either side, in haze, yet plainly defin'd, giant brothers twain, throwing free graceful interlinking loops high across the tumbled tumultuous current below . . . ."

Hart Crane's masterpiece, "The Bridge," is an epic poem built around the image of the Brooklyn Bridge and the future it predicted. In 1924 Crane, one of America's great prophetic poets, lived in the same building where Washington Roebling had lived, and looked out on the bridge every day. "Every time one looks at the harbor and the New York skyline across the river it is quite different," he wrote. He finished the poem on December 26, 1929. Three years later, while returning to New York from a trip to Mexico, Crane committed suicide by jumping from the deck of his ship.

Poet **Marianne Moore**, who lived in Brooklyn for years, liked to take the Manhattan Bridge into the city so that she could better see the Brooklyn Bridge "silhouetted by the sun or the moon." **Thomas Wolfe** described the bridge's "wing-like sweep." **Arthur Miller** said that it was the most beautiful structure he had ever seen. **John Dos Passos**, a friend of Hart Crane, wrote about the bridge, as did **Lewis Mumford, Jack Kerouac, Allen Ginsberg,** and **Caleb Carr. Henry James** is probably the only writer who hated the bridge—he saw it as a mechanical monster drawing the world closer together, making it smaller, not better. The Brooklyn Bridge did not just inspire American writers. **Vladimir Mayakovsky** and **Federico García Lorca** both admired and wrote about it, as well. Paintings by John Marin and Joseph Stella and countless photographs have further immortalized the bridge.

Brooklyn Bridge

St. Luke's Place

St. Luke's Place between Hudson Street and Seventh Avenue

Less than a block long, picturesque St. Luke's Place has houses only on one side of the street. Yet it was the home to more writers of note than entire neighborhoods elsewhere. As you walk west on St. Luke's Place from Seventh Avenue, the first building of importance is No. 16. This was the house in which **Theodore Dreiser** (1871–1945) lived from 1922 to 1923, when he wrote his masterpiece, *An American Tragedy*. He was in a constant battle against censors who thought his works like *Sister Carrie* (1900) had too vividly described the seamier sides of life. On one occasion, his supporters—**F. Scott Fitzgerald**, **Horace Liveright**, **H .L. Mencken**, and **Carl Van Vechten**—held a meeting here on the parlor floor to discuss strategies for overcoming the censorship of his work. Though Dreiser lived at many different addresses in New York City, he began *An American Tragedy* here and completed it in an office he rented at 201 Park Avenue South. It is fitting to include him with the other literary legends on the block. Dreiser went on to become a key figure in the American naturalist movement, developing a commitment to social reform and later joining the Communist

St. Luke's Place

Party in 1945, the same year in which he died.

From 1918 until 1929, No. 14 was the home of poet
Marianne Moore (1887–1972), one of a group of writers known as The Others. She arrived in New York
City after teaching at the Carlisle Indian School
in Pennsylvania for several years and found a
job across the street at the Hudson Park
Branch of the New York Public Library. Moore
lived in the basement apartment with her mother

F. Scott Fitzgerald

and wrote poetry in her spare time. In 1924, she won the Dial Award for
her book *Observations*, and the following year, she went to work as an
editor for *Dial*, one of the most important literary magazines of the time.
In 1929, she left the magazine to devote all her energy to writing and
moved with her mother to the Fort Greene section of Brooklyn. She lived
there for many years until her mother's death, then returned to the Village, living not far from St. Luke's Place, at 35 West 9th Street. In
1951—Moore's best year—she published her *Collected Poems*, which
won the National Book Award, the Pulitzer Prize and the Bollingen
Prize. Besides being well-known as a poet, she was also an avid baseball
fan and could often be seen at Brooklyn Dodger games with her trade-
mark three-cornered hat and cape.

Sherwood Anderson (1876-1941), the author of *Winesburg, Ohio*, lived
at No. 12 St. Luke's Place just a few doors away from Dreiser and also
attended the meeting in support of Dreiser in 1922. Anderson was
awestruck by Dreiser's reputation. When Anderson moved to St. Luke's
Place, he knew that Dreiser was his neighbor but was too shy to intro-
duce himself. He wrote about approaching Dreiser's door several times
before gathering the courage to knock, after several days of hesitation.
When Dreiser saw Anderson, he said hello and closed the door in his
face. Later that day, Dreiser sent Anderson a note of apology explaining
that he, too, had been awestruck and was embarrassed to speak to
Anderson. Soon after, they became friends.

Edna St. Vincent Millay's House

75 1/2 Bedford Street between Commerce and Morton Streets

Known as the "narrowest house in New York," 75 1/2 Bedford Street is also honored with a plaque commemorating **Edna St. Vincent Millay**, who resided here for a short while in 1923 to 1924. Millay, named after St. Vincent's Hospital in New York's Greenwich Village, was born in Rockland, Maine, in 1892. She showed early promise as a poet and upon graduation from Vassar she moved to the Village in 1917. Millay was an exceptional beauty and supported herself as an actress, first with the Theatre Guild and then at the Provincetown Playhouse. She directed two of her own plays at the Provincetown Playhouse and continued to write poetry, including her most famous lines:

> My candle burns at both ends:
> It will not last the night;
> But ah, my foes, and oh, my friends
> It gives a lovely light.

Millay was a woman who thought for herself, took lovers on her own terms and did as she pleased, a half century before the women's liberation movement. One of her paramours was Edmund Wilson. He helped her gain the attention of *Vanity Fair*, and during the early 1920s she became one of their most popular writers. In 1923, Millay returned from two years in Paris, married Eugen Boissevain, and moved into this tiny house on Bedford Street. While here

Edna St. Vincent Millay's house

she received the Pulitzer Prize for *The Ballad of the Harp Weaver*, a collection of her poems that helped define the era. She also collaborated with Deems Taylor on an American opera entitled *The King's Henchman*. After leaving New York City, she lived and wrote at her home, "Steepletop," in Austerlitz, New York, until her death in 1950. The six-hundred-acre farm was then turned into the Millay Colony for the Arts, an artist's retreat that still attracts creative artists, composers and writers.

Edna St. Vincent Millay

This house also has a certain fame beyond Millay. The building appears in the movie, *Bachelor Party*, and was also the home of John Barrymore, Margaret Mead, William Steig, and Cary Grant for short periods of time. It seems that the house is just too claustrophobic for anything but short-term residence.

Chumley's

86 Bedford Street between Grove and Barrow Streets

Chumley's is the most famous "secret" spot in New York, one of the few bars in the city to remain unchanged from Prohibition (1920–33) and the speakeasies that resulted. After the White Horse, Chumley's is the oldest literary watering hole in the Village. Lee Chumley opened the place in 1928, and it has attracted a bohemian crowd to its small, cozy rooms ever since. Chumley died in 1935, but his wife Henrietta continued running the bar for the next twenty-five years. Actually the bar more or less ran itself, while Mrs. Chumley sat next to the fireplace, sampling the goods until she was finally taken home each night. One night in 1960 the waiters couldn't rouse her from her stupor and found she had died at the table during the evening.

No one would suspect that behind the rather formidable door with the iron grille is a warm, friendly tavern. No sign is visible and there has never been one in its long history. Although today the main entrance is at 86 Bedford Street, there is another entrance from Barrow Street. In speakeasy days, customers would enter through the backyard, called Pamela Court, at 58 Barrow Street. The door at 86 Bedford Street was

Chumley's

used only as the patrons' escape route during police raids. While Chumley held back the cops, the patrons were warned to "eighty-six it," meaning to clear out fast through the other door, hence the birth of a new term.

Without commenting on why writers gravitate to saloons and bars—let's just say that they do—this bar has seen more than its share. Over the years it has been frequented by the likes of **Djuna Barnes, William S. Burroughs, John Cheever, e.e.**

Dylan Thomas

cummings, Simone de Beauvoir, John Dos Passos, Theodore Dreiser, William Faulkner, Edna Ferber, Lawrence Ferlinghetti, F. Scott Fitzgerald, Allen Ginsberg, Ernest Hemingway, Jack Kerouac, Sinclair Lewis, Mary McCarthy, Edna St. Vincent Millay, Arthur Miller, Anaïs Nin, Eugene O'Neill, J.D. Salinger, Upton Sinclair, John Steinbeck, Dylan Thomas, Orson Welles, Thornton Wilder, and **Edmund Wilson**. Quite a roster for a place without a sign.

On the walls you'll find book covers from the bar's many writer customers. Over the years they've added more and more layers of book jackets, and they still can't keep up. It's a popular literary rendezvous spot for a very literate neighborhood.

Grove Court

Grove Street between Bedford and Hudson Streets

Grove Court is a charming hidden courtyard, located on Grove Street between Bedford and Hudson streets. The wrought iron gate is between numbers 10 and 12 Grove, and although usually locked, the buildings can easily be seen from the street. The brick Greek Revival homes were built for working-class families between 1853 and 1854, when space was becoming scarce and buildings were filling every nook and cranny in the Village. This lane was originally a slum known as Mixed Ale Alley, proba-

Grove Court

bly due to the drinking habits of the residents and later called Pig Alley. In 1921, it became the more genteel Grove Court.

In 1902, **O. Henry**'s daughter is believed to have lived here and the writer's famous short story, "The Last Leaf" was conceived here. "The Last Leaf" is the story of Sue and Johnsy, two young girls who come to New York to find fame and fortune as artists. Pneumonia strikes Johnsy and the doctor gives her little hope for survival. She loses the will to live, and from her sick bed she watches the leaves drop one by one from an ivy vine growing on the wall outside her garret window. She believes that when she sees the last leaf fall from the vine, she will die. On the first floor lives a kindly old neighbor, Mr. Behrman, also an artist. He has spent his whole life painting without any real success and dreams of the day when he will create his masterpiece. On the night that the last leaf falls during a raging storm, the old man climbs a ladder and paints a leaf onto the vine. Each morning the young girl awakes to see that the one single leaf remains steadfast, and with each day she recovers a little more of her strength. In the meantime, Mr. Behrman suffers from the effects of being soaked to the bone in the cold rain and dies of pneumonia.

What was once dangerous and dirty due to its secluded, backyard location is now considered a quaint address in Greenwich Village, sheltered from the bustle and whirl of the city.

St. Luke-in-the-Field

487 Hudson Street at Grove Street

Clement Clarke Moore (1779–1863), theologian, professor of classical linguistics, philanthropist, and once the owner of most of the property that is today known as Chelsea, was described as "the kindliest of scholars, the most assiduous of bookworms, a writer whose works were held in high regard by the learned men of his day." Yet he is best known as the author of a little poem that he wrote solely to amuse his six children in 1822.

While riding in a sleigh on his way back to his home in Greenwich Village, he composed "A Visit from St. Nicholas," which begins with the line "Twas the night before Christmas." If a friend hadn't secretly mailed the poem to the *Troy Sentinel*, where it was published the following year, we might never have heard of Santa Claus popping down the chimney from his sleigh and eight tiny reindeer, all inventions of Moore.

At the time he wrote the poem, Moore was the first warden and vestryman of the newly built St. Luke's Episcopal Chapel of Trinity Parish, now known as St. Luke-in-the-Field. The cornerstone for the building was laid in 1821 and work completed the following year. At that time the church overlooked small farms and the tiny Greenwich Village. Although Moore trained for the

Letter from N. Tuttle to Clement C. Moore concerning the authorship of "A Visit from St. Nicholas"

ministry after graduating from Columbia, he never took orders, instead devoting himself to teaching. Moore's family mansion was near the current intersection of Ninth Avenue and West 23rd Street, but in the winter he lived on Charlton Street. In the 1830s, Moore donated land for the General Theological Seminary on Ninth Avenue and helped design and build St. Peter's Episcopal Church on West 20th Street, both in Chelsea.

He is buried in Trinity Cemetery, the rural cemetery for Trinity Church, in Washington Heights near West 155th Street, where each Christmas Eve children gather in a candlelight procession to sing carols and hear his most famous poem read aloud. Clement Clarke Moore Park on the corner of Tenth Avenue and West 22nd Street also pays tribute to Moore.

St. Luke-in-the-Field

White Horse Tavern

567 Hudson Street at West 11th Street

The oldest and most famous literary bar in Greenwich Village is the White Horse Tavern at 567 Hudson Street. Built in 1880 as a seaman's bar, it is one of the few wood-framed buildings remaining in Manhattan. The White Horse is also the third oldest bar in the city and during Prohibition became a speakeasy. In the late 1940s it began to gain a literary reputation and by the 1950s it had replaced the San Remo as the literary hangout of choice in the Village.

Norman Mailer, **Dan Wolf**, and **Ed Fancher**, who later founded the *Village Voice* together, began a Sunday afternoon tradition of meeting at the White Horse as early as 1951. They liked the quiet neighborhood quality of the place. Writers like political activist **Michael Harrington**, critic **John Aldridge**, and novelist **John Clellon Holmes** began frequenting the bar. Even non-Village writers like **Louis Auchincloss**, poets **Delmore Schwartz**, **Lawrence Ferlinghetti**, and **Herman Wouk** occasionally visited the White Horse.

But the writer most frequently associated with the White Horse Tavern remains the great Welsh poet **Dylan Thomas**. Fellow authors, **Ruthven Todd** and **John Malcolm Brinnin**, first brought him to the White Horse on one of his American reading tours. Thomas made the bar his not-so-private clubhouse during all his stays in New York. He drank heavily here each night including the night in 1953 when he died from alcoholism at age thirty-eight. There is a room to the left of the bar dedicated to his memory and filled with pictures and posters of Thomas.

White Horse Tavern

Irish writer **Brendan Behan** followed in Thomas's footsteps, stopping at the White Horse whenever he was in New York City. He was not alone. **Jane Jacobs** mentions the bar prominently in her 1961 book, *The Death and Life of Great American Cities*, and **William Styron**, **Vance Bourjaily**, and **Frederic Morton** have visited from time to time, as well. **Jack Kerouac** and his Beat Generation friends hung around the White Horse, too. Here, as elsewhere, Kerouac drank too much and was kicked out several times. Once he found "Kerouac, go home!" scrawled on the men's room wall. In *Desolation Angels* he describes being dragged out of the bar by his girlfriend, author **Joyce Johnson**, in a fit of jealousy.

The old wooden barroom has barely changed since Kerouac's day; a few extra side rooms have been added and in the summer there is outdoor seating along the sidewalk. The best times to visit are in the afternoons, for a quiet drink, or in the evenings, for a more active bar scene.

Thomas Paine's Last Home

59 Grove Street at Seventh Avenue

One of the early champions of American independence was Englishman **Thomas Paine** (1737–1809) who arrived in the colonies from England in 1774, just two years before the beginning of the Revolution. Through his pamphlet *Common Sense*, published in January of 1776, he spoke for freedom and democracy to a group of colonists tired of European tyranny. This single pamphlet did more than any other writing to ignite the revolutionary feelings of the common people and sway public opinion towards the cause of independence.

Late in 1776, he published his famous pamphlet *The Crisis*, which bolstered the sagging morale of the colonial forces at Valley Forge. Beginning with the lines "These are the times that try men's souls: The summer soldier and the sunshine patriot will, in this crisis, shrink from the service of his country; but he that stands it now, deserves the love and thanks of man and woman," *The Crisis* turned Paine into a hero of the people and throughout the Revolution he wrote articles extolling the virtues of liberty. President John Adams wrote, "I know not whether any man in the world has had more influence on its inhabitants or affairs for the last thirty years than Thomas Paine."

During the Revolution, Paine lived in Philadelphia. In 1787, he went to France and stayed for fifteen years to observe the French Revolution and its aftermath, the Reign of Terror. In 1792 he wrote *The Rights of Man* and in 1807, *The Age of Reason*. In honor of this book, Barrow Street was called Reason Street. Soon after, however, the public began to identify Paine with the excesses of the French Revolution, and he was charged with blasphemy by church groups.

In 1803, Paine returned to New Rochelle, New York, and settled on a farm that had been given to him by the State Assembly in honor of his patriotic deeds during the Revolution. It was not a happy retirement, as more and more people grew to hate him for his opposition to the Federalists and all organized religions; even his old friends would not visit him. He grew sick and returned to New York City, living in several houses in the Village. The month of his death, he begged an old friend from Paris, Marguerite de Bonneville, to take him in. Reluctantly, she rented him a house at 59 Grove Street next to her own and nursed him until he died on June 8, 1809. There is a plaque today on the house built in 1839 that

Thomas Paine

replaced the wooden frame house near the corner of Seventh Avenue. The marker quotes Paine: "The world is my country, all mankind are my brethren, to do good is my religion, I believe in one God and no more." The plaque is affixed next to the front door of Marie's Crisis, a cabaret named by its first owner Marie Dumont, in honor of Paine's great pamphlet, *The Crisis*.

At his death, the great patriot was stripped of his American citizenship. His last request was to be buried in a Quaker churchyard, but the church refused. During the intervening years, his bones were lost, and when the church relented, Paine's remains could not be located. Some people believe that friends secretly interred the bones in a churchyard without permission.

My Sister Eileen's House

14 Gay Street between Christopher Street and Waverly Place

One of the shortest streets in the Village also houses a secret literary landmark. Gay Street is not much more than an alley connecting Christopher Street and Waverly Place and in the 1930s, it was just another run-down address for struggling artists and writers. At No. 14 Gay Street is the basement apartment that **Ruth McKenney** and her sister, Eileen, moved into when they arrived from Ohio in 1935. Seeking fame and fortune in the big city, Ruth wanted to be a writer and her younger sister, an actress. Everything was an adventure for the two girls, from the walls that shook due to subway construction, to casting calls; from cat burglars, to adventures with a group of Brazilian naval cadets down the street. Ruth began writing about their humorous exploits for the *New Yorker*, where they became known as "My Sister Eileen" stories, gaining in popularity with each new adventure. By 1938, there were enough stories to make a book, and *My Sister Eileen* was published, quickly becoming a best-seller.

The book captured the heart of America, and spread the idea of Greenwich Village—with its zany cast of bohemian characters—as the place for up and coming talent. The stories were a natural for the theater, and a Broadway play based on the book opened on December 26, 1940. *My Sister Eileen* was again a hit, and it ran for two years, starring Shirley Booth as Ruth and JoAnn Sayers as Eileen. But the popularity of these two sisters did not end there; in 1942, the movie version of the play was made with Rosalind Russell as Ruth, Janet Blair as Eileen and Brian Aherne playing the part of the boyfriend. In 1953, the play was turned into a musical called *Wonderful Town*, with a score by Leonard Bernstein and lyrics by Betty Comden and Adolph Green, with Rosalind

"My Sister Eileen," with Jo Ann Sayers, Shirley Booth, and Morris Carnovsky

Russell appearing again as Ruth. The public continued to thrilled with the story and *Wonderful Town* became one of Broadway's biggest hits. One more movie version was made in 1955, this one in color (the original had been in black and white), starring Betty Garrett, Janet Leigh, and Jack Lemmon. Finally, *Wonderful Town* was made into a television special in 1958, with Russell once more playing the role of Ruth McKenney.

With all the success these triumphs brought Ruth McKenney, she was not without personal tragedy. In 1940, just a few days before the Broadway opening of the play, her sister Eileen was killed in a car accident along with her new husband, writer **Nathanael West**. He had just written *The Day of the Locust*, and their life together was full of promise. McKenney's later writings never equaled the popularity of *My Sister Eileen*. The building the McKenneys lived in has changed little on the outside since those days. Among the other notable residents of this street have been the creator of Howdy Doody, Frank Parris, who lived at No. 12, as did a mistress of Mayor James Walker, Betty Compton. Across the street, the activist-lawyer William Kunstler had his office.

Mary McCarthy's Apartment
18 Gay Street between Christopher Street and Waverly Place

With a $25-a-week allowance from her grandfather, **Mary McCarthy** (1912–1989) moved to a single room in the building at 18 Gay Street in 1936. It was to be a pivotal point that helped shape her life and as a result, figures prominently in her very autobiographical books. Just a few years earlier, in 1933, McCarthy had graduated from Vassar, moved to New York City, married Harold Johnsrud, quickly divorced and begun a literary career that would reach its zenith with the publication of *The Group* in 1963. That book tells the story of eight friends, all from Vassar's Class of '33, who came to New York to find careers, romance, and freedom from the bonds of more conservative lifestyles. It was this liberating approach to life that made *The Group* an instant best-seller and the novel's heroines became role models for a new generation of American women.

As liberated as she was, McCarthy never felt fulfilled in her own life, however. After the first failed marriage, she took a series of lovers, always on her own terms. She had a famous affair with **Philip Rahv**, editor of the *Partisan Review*, and recounted the details in her book *Intellectual Memoirs: New York 1936–1938*. She described her room on Gay Street carefully in that book. "The one room apartment I moved into on Gay Street had eleven sides. I counted one day when I was sick in bed. The normal quota, including floor and ceiling, would have been six. But my little place had many jogs, many irregularities. There was a tiny kitchen and bath suited to a bird. Another amusing oddity of the apartment was that, small as it was, it had two street entrances: one on Gay Street and one, leading through a passageway, to Christopher Street, where the bells and mailboxes were." She said that her circle of friends shrank along with her move to the tiny apartment. In 1941 *Partisan Review* published her story "The Man in the Brooks Brothers Shirt" which tells of an affair between a young woman and an older man on a cross-country train. Later the man visited McCarthy on Gay Street, took her to a World Series game and urged her to move. Jay Laughlin of New Directions, helped spread the rumor that the man was Wendell Willkie, who had been a Republican candidate for president in 1940. Decades later McCarthy identified the man, not as Willkie, but as George Black from Pittsburgh. It wasn't the last time that a scandal was to be connected with McCarthy. In 1979, during an interview on the Dick Cavett Show, McCarthy took aim at **Lillian Hellman** and declared her "tremendously overrated, a bad writer and a dishonest writer." Hellman filed a lawsuit against McCarthy and a nasty battle took place not only in court but on the pages of the tabloids as well. This fight had been brewing since McCarthy's earlier *Partisan Review* days when she had helped steer the magazine's editorial policies away from a Stalinist position, which was supported by Hellman, towards a Trotskyite form of socialist theory, which McCarthy herself favored.

During her life, McCarthy lived at various places in the city according to her financial and marital status at the time. She had an apartment at 2 Beekman Place with her first husband, which she decorated with borrowed furniture. The couple was always behind in the rent, and a kindly rental agent let them stay on for months. After living on Gay Street, McCarthy moved back to Beekman Place with Philip Rahv into a borrowed apartment. Although an important partner in her life, they never married. In the end she did have four husbands, one son, and a large assortment of lovers, both serious and not. Through it all, McCarthy was always at the center of New York's literary and intellectual life, even though she lived much of her life outside the city.

Pfaff's Cellar

647 Broadway near Bleecker Street

Perhaps the writer most identified with nineteenth-century New York City, **Walt Whitman** (1819–1892), is also the most difficult to attach to a particular site. Surprisingly, nearly every site associated with Walt Whitman's forty years in New York City is now gone. Why no statues or plaques commemorate his life in the city is a mystery, since his poetry extols the city more than the work of any other writer. He enthusiastically embraced the city, its inhabitants, and even the very progress that has wiped out his shadow. Newspapers for which he worked prospered and moved to larger and more modern quarters or failed and were replaced by newer build-

ings. Scholars Paul Berman, Eli Wilentz, and Sean Wilentz have discovered that one of the Brooklyn houses built and lived in by Whitman in 1848 still exists. At 99 Ryerson Street, the old house is still lurking behind a renovated facade.

Early edition of
Walt Whitman's *Leaves of Grass*

In Manhattan, only the building in which his favorite saloon, Pfaff's, was located has survived. Several writers have reported various addresses for Pfaff's, but the New York Historical Society found that 647 Broadway was the true location of the cellar in which Pfaff's operated. It was in this beer cellar that author and editor, **William Dean Howells** first met Whitman in 1860, though Howells did not drink. An early biographer wrote of their meeting: "Whitman, white-haired and bearded, looking closer to eighty than forty, wearing an open-necked shirt and a homespun suit, is leaning back in his chair and casually shaking hands with a young, slim, formally dressed Howells, who is bending slightly toward the poet, as though paying court. Howells later came to understand Whitman, the rough poet of New York's streets, in terms of his own Boston-adopted gentility: 'The apostle of the rough, the uncouth, was the gentlest person; his barbaric yawp, translated into the terms of social encounter, was an address of singular quiet, delivered in a voice of winning and endearing friendliness.'"

After a short teaching stint, Whitman began working for various newspapers. He took the ferry back and forth to work every day, hence the inspiration for one of his more famous poems, "Crossing Brooklyn Ferry," from his collection *Leaves of Grass* (1855).

During the years when he frequented Pfaff's tavern, Whitman was the editor of the *Brooklyn Eagle*, but he resigned in 1847 over a dispute with the publisher. He became friends with **Ralph Waldo Emerson** and other Concord, Massachusetts, luminaries such as **Henry Thoreau** and **Bronson Alcott**, and in the process alienated himself from New York's literary establishment. He moved to Camden, New Jersey, and continued to write until his death in 1892.

Pfaff's Cellar   Walt Whitman

San Remo Bar

189 Bleecker Street at MacDougal Street

The bohemian lifestyle that helped define the personality of 1940s and '50s Greenwich Village was centered around the coffeehouses and cheap bars near the intersection of MacDougal and Bleecker Streets. Their great attraction has always been the seemingly unlimited amount of time a patron could spend inside. During the early 1900s, the neighborhood became predominantly Italian and European-style coffeehouses sprang up on every corner. The Village began to attract more and more hipsters, bohemians, and free-thinkers from all over the world, and they gravitated towards these places because they were inexpensive and their owners didn't mind their offbeat habits.

The literary crowd's most famous hangout in this area was on the northwest corner of MacDougal and Bleecker Streets at the San Remo, now called Carpo's Cafe. Joe Santini opened the San Remo in 1923 and it remained a thriving hangout well into the 1950s. Its wooden booths, pressed tin ceiling, and black and white tile floors no longer remain after decades of remodeling. Nor do the "bad yellowed paintings over the bar" recalled by

William S. Burroughs and Alan Ansen outside San Remo, 1953

writer **Michael Harrington**, who went there every night upon his arrival from Chicago in 1949. The San Remo hosted quite a mix of people, which was part of its appeal. Besides writers and artists, there were sailors, laborers, homosexuals, communists, drug addicts, and the occasional tourist from Iowa. Many of the greatest talents of the era spent

time in the San Remo, including **James Agee, James Baldwin, William S. Burroughs, John Cage, Gregory Corso, Merce Cunningham, Miles Davis, William Gaddis, Paul Goodman, John Clellon Holmes, Norman Mailer, Frank O'Hara, Jackson Pollock, Larry Rivers, William Styron, Dylan Thomas, Gore Vidal,** and **Tennessee Williams**.

The San Remo was the center of **Jack Kerouac**'s New York social life for several years. It figures prominently in his novel *The Subterraneans*, in which he renamed it "The Mask" and moved it to San Francisco to disguise the fact that he was writing about real people. Kerouac's best friend, **Allen Ginsberg**, had coined the term "subterraneans" to describe the alienated and disaffected bohemians who hung out in places like the San Remo, one of the starting spots for his nightly antics with his Beat Generation friends. The popularity of the place declined when its tough bartenders began to beat up customers and the hipsters moved elsewhere.

Judith Malina and Julian Beck first conceived the idea of The Living Theatre through all-night conversations they had at the San Remo. The writer Maxwell Bodenheim, a village character and a colorful writer, hung out there cadging drinks. It was also one of the favorite haunts of the intellectual bum, Joe Gould, also known as Professor Seagull, who gained notoriety when *New Yorker* writer Joe Mitchell published a series of articles about him.

Provincetown Playhouse

133 MacDougal Street between West Third and Fourth Streets

The Provincetown Playhouse began in 1915 when a group of New Yorkers vacationing in Provincetown, Massachusetts, at the tip of Cape Cod, decided to stage one act plays on the porch of their summer home. The plays met with some success, so the group moved into a makeshift theater on a nearby wharf in 1916. That year they produced *Bound East for Cardiff*, by the then unknown writer, **Eugene O'Neill** (1888–1953), who had a whole trunk filled with plays for them to stage. The players were encouraged enough by their first success to open an amateur theater in the Village when they returned that fall. They rented a room at 139 MacDougal Street, next to Polly's and the Liberal Club, and the next year moved to a larger space—an old stable at 133 MacDougal. They produced most of O'Neill's early works, and in 1920 had their greatest success with his *The Emperor Jones*, which moved to Broadway and established O'Neill as one of the greatest playwrights of his time. The play, one of the first for a white audience featuring a black actor in the lead, Charles Gilpin, was unprecedented and controversial. When it opened in London, Paul Robeson played the role of Brutus Jones. In 1924, Robeson premiered at the Provincetown Playhouse in O'Neill's controversial, *All God's Chillun Got Wings*. One critic wrote, "Before O'Neill, the United States had theater, after O'Neill, it had drama." O'Neill is the only American playwright to win the Nobel Prize for Literature, in addition to his four Pulitzer Prizes.

O'Neill lived in various cheap rooming houses around the Village, including at least two on Washington Square South, and spent most of his time at the Golden Swan, a bar on Sixth Avenue known as the "Hell

Hole." He turned his experiences and the people he knew there into *The Iceman Cometh*. His dramas are intense psychological studies of insanity, alcoholism, passion, and depression. He used his life as the basis for most of his work—his affair with John Reed's wife, Louise Bryant, was the origin of his *Strange Interlude*.

Over the years other Villagers joined the growing theatrical group. **John Reed**, one of the original founders, helped draw up the Provincetown Players' constitution. **e. e. cummings** wrote a controversial play called *him* premiered by the Provincetown Players. **Edna St. Vincent Millay** acted in several plays and wrote two. The Players produced plays by Maxwell Bodenheim and Alfred Kreymborg. Bette Davis, Ann Harding and Miriam Hopkins began their acting careers with the Players. In 1929 the group known as the Provincetown Players gave their final performance. **Edward Albee**'s play, *The Zoo Story*, was first produced in 1960 in the new Provincetown Theater built on the old site.

Eugene O'Neill

Washington Square

*Washington Square North and South
from MacDougal to University Place*

It is impossible to describe briefly the literary significance of the homes surrounding this small patch of New York greenery. Occasionally, buildings are found in the city which have been the home for two or three celebrated writers; here and there are streets on which five or six writers lived. But on Washington Square the crush of genius is overwhelming. Dozens upon dozens of notable persons have lived, worked, studied, played, dined, and drank in this immediate vicinity. If Greenwich Village was the mecca for the avant-garde in New York City, then Washington Square was the focal point of the Village. Where else in America can you sit on a park bench knowing that nearby were once the homes and offices of **Willa Cather**, **Stephen Crane**, **John Dos Passos**, **William Dean Howells**, **Henry James**, **Joyce Kilmer**, **O. Henry**, **Eugene O'Neill**, **Edgar Allan Poe**, **Upton**

Willa Cather

Sinclair, **Sara Teasdale**, **Walt Whitman**, and **Thomas Wolfe**, to name only a very few? Merely listing each person would make this chapter the longest in the book, so a selective sample might help.

On both sides of Fifth Avenue are long blocks of beautiful townhouses that were called simply "The Row." The Landmarks Preservation Commission considers the beautiful buildings at Nos. 1–13 to the east of Fifth Avenue to be "the most important and imposing block front of early nineteenth-century town houses in the city." They were built from 1832–33 as single family dwellings for the wealthiest New York merchants and bankers. Behind the houses on Washington Mews and Mac-Dougal Alley were carriage houses and stables for these residents, and if you walk along the alleyways today you'll find it a charming and relaxing retreat. Some of the buildings of "The Row" have been altered, and a few on the west corner of Fifth Avenue have been replaced by a modern apartment building. At Nos. 7–13, on the east side of Fifth Avenue, renovators gutted the buildings for new apartments, which are entered from the Fifth Avenue side, but the facades facing the park remain intact. Washington Square North is so closely associated with Henry James and Edith Wharton and the lifestyle they described in their books, that it would be a mistake to start anywhere else.

Edith Wharton (1862–1937) was born in a house that still stands at 14 West 23rd Street, but in her book, *The Age of Innocence*, she wrote about events set in the 1870s, when Washington Square would have been the very center of New York's high society. Wharton was from a

prominent family and lived in a world where people "always lived well, dressed expensively, and did little else," as she described in *The House of Mirth*. Her books dealt with the shifting of old-family quiet wealth to the excesses of the more cosmopolitan Gilded Age. Wharton lived at No. 7 for a short while after her father's death in 1881, when she returned to New York City from Europe. She was the first woman to win the Pulitzer Prize.

Edith Wharton

49

"The Row" was also the setting for the novel *Washington Square*, by Wharton's closest friend, **Henry James** (1843–1916). It was made into the classic film "The Heiress" starring Olivia de Havilland as the plain but wealthy daughter, Catherine Sloper, with Ralph Richardson as her cruel father and Montgomery Clift as the gold digger determined to win the daughter's heart and purse. The aristocratic New Yorkers James immortalized were based on the people living here. Henry James was born a block from Washington Square at 21 Washington Place, in a house that is no longer standing. James's grandmother lived on "The Row" to the west of Fifth Avenue, at No. 18, and although that house is no longer there either, the remaining homes west of it, from No. 19 on, are so similar that you'll get an idea of what it was like in James's day. He wrote *Washington Square* while he was living in England in 1881, but relied heavily on his childhood memories of her house.

More recent inhabitants of "The Row" have been more radical in politics and art. They have included John Dos Passos, who wrote *Manhattan Transfer* while living at No. 3. Later, inhabitants of the same building included **Edmund Wilson, Rockwell Kent, William Glackens, John Sloan,** and **Edward Hopper,** who died here in 1966. America's first professionally trained architect, Richard Morris Hunt, lived at No.

Washington Square, looking north

2. John Taylor Johnston, one of the founders of the Metropolitan Museum of Art, was born at No. 7. **Edward Cooper**, New York City's Mayor from 1878–80 lived at No. 8. **William Dean Howells**, the author of *The Rise of Silas Lapham*, lived at No. 1.

While practically everything on the north side of Washington Square spoke of an aristocratic, fashionably elite society, everything on Washington Square South reflected the other side of the coin. Here, homes were turned into cheap boardinghouses crammed with the poor artists and writers who crowded into Greenwich Village to experiment

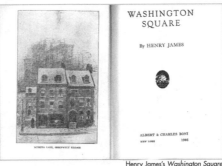

Henry James's *Washington Square*

with the bohemian lifestyle. While the patriarchs of old New York families managed to hang on to their wealth and homes along the North and thus preserved them, the buildings on the south side fell into disrepair and were torn down, replaced and torn down again. Today, no remnants of that boardinghouse life remain facing the park. Some of the old tenements can still be seen on the surrounding streets but they have been improved. Although the buildings are gone, it is still important to remember the history here before New York University bought all the real estate in this part of the city.

NYU is building a new student center on the southwest corner of Washington Square South and La Guardia Place. Several buildings existed on this site, but the most important was a rooming house at No. 61 that came to be known as "The House of Genius." This was owned by Madame Katarina Branchard. Besides running a rickety, ratty, dirty boarding house, she had a soft spot for creative people. Among the occupants were poet Gelett Burgess, whose nonsense rhymes like "I Never Saw a Purple Crane" became extremely popular; **Stephen Crane** wrote his most famous book, *The Red Badge of Courage*, while staying here; Theodore Dreiser was possibly a visitor here—he lived in so many apartments in the city that it's difficult to be certain; **Zona Gale** lived here, as did **Amy Lowell**; **Frank Norris** moved here in 1899 and began work on *The Octopus*; **James Oppenheim** stayed here as did **Alan**

Seeger, who wrote the prophetic poem "I Have a Rendezvous with Death," and was killed on the battlefield during World War I. **Upton Sinclair** also lived and wrote in "The House of Genius." They all stayed here as struggling authors, and they all moved out as their circumstances improved. Even the inventor of the Kewpie Doll lived here in 1909. **Madame Branchard** died in 1937 at the age of eighty-one and the building was torn down in 1948.

Next door at No. 60, Willa Cather roomed, as did her friend Edith Lewis, who later wrote a biography of Cather. After the success of her 1913 book, *O Pioneers!*, Cather moved to her own place at 5 Bank Street where she lived until 1927. During that time she wrote her best known work, *My Antonia*, and won a Pulitzer Prize for *One of Ours* in 1922.

Andy Brown, Marianne Moore, Frances Steloff and Ted Wilentz

Sherwood Anderson

Another popular boarding-house, nicknamed "Parnassas Flats," stood at No. 42. **John Reed** wrote a poem titled "The Day in Bohemia: Or, Life Among the Artists" about his life there in 1913. Reed's friend and fellow writer, Lincoln Steffens, also lived in the samebuilding. Steffens made Reed aware of the deplorable social conditions of the common man and this prompted him to cover the Russian Revolution. This decision changed his brief life drastically.

A small tea room called Polly's Restaurant was the central meeting place for a group of liberal intellectuals in the 1910s. It was in the basement of a building that once stood near the corner of MacDougal Street and Washington Square South at 137 MacDougal, and among the people who gathered here and at The Liberal Club upstairs were anarchists like **Emma Goldman** and **Hippolyte Havel**, writers **Sherwood Anderson, Theodore Dreiser, Max Eastman, Sinclair Lewis, Vachel Lindsay, Upton Sinclair, Lincoln Steffens**, and **Louis Untermeyer.** Here they began work on the magazine, *The Masses*, which became the most liberal political and literary periodical of the time. Next door to Polly's was the Washington Square Book Shop, which gave birth to Boni and Liveright Publishers as well as the Modern Library. Writers associated with the magazine *Others* also hung out at Polly's. **Maxwell Bodenheim, Alfred Kreymborg, Marianne Moore, Wallace Stevens**, and **William Carlos Williams** were all regulars. Each new generation has reinvented Washington Square and the Village, and so it continues today.

Patchin Place

West 10th Street between Sixth and Greenwich Avenues

A peacefully quiet cul-de-sac, which contrasts sharply with the hustle and bustle of the nearby avenues, would be a welcome place to mention even if it were not the home of several of New York City's most important literary figures. It is easy to miss the entrance to Patchin Place on the north side of West 10th Street between Sixth Avenue and Greenwich Avenue, but once you've spotted it, you won't forget where it is. The ten simple houses on both sides of the tiny street were built for working-class people in 1848 by Aaron D. Patchin. At that time, wealthier people preferred larger homes right on the major thoroughfares.

Edward Estlin Cummings (1894–1962), who is better known as e.e. cummings, eschewed uppercase letters and punctuation and established spacing and meter to create a unique form of personal poetry in the 1920s. He lived at No. 4 Patchin Place from 1923 until his death in 1962. He shared a room here with his third wife, photographer and fashion model Marion Morehouse, and together they acquired more and more of the house until they had all but one room on the third floor. Morehouse and cummings were very sociable, and they entertained many famous guests, including **T. S. Eliot**, **Ezra Pound**, **John Dos Passos**, and one night, a very drunken **Dylan Thomas**. Dos Passos remembered that they'd go out for supper

T. S. Eliot

54

together, then drinks, and the more they drank, the more cummings would talk. "It was as if he were spouting pages of prose and verse from an unwritten volume. Then suddenly he would go off to Patchin Place to put some of it down before the fountain ceased to flow." His early work was not immediately accepted for publication, but luckily, he had a small amount of personal money with which he was able to publish his first books. Cummings went on to receive many awards during his lifetime, from the Dial Award in 1925 to his election to the National Institute of Arts and Letters in the 1950s. When asked why he continued to live in Patchin Place, cummings wrote "because here's friend-ly. unscientific. pri-vate. human."

In sharp contrast to cummings's outgoing and gregarious nature, his neighbor across the way in a single room at No. 5 was reclusive to the extreme. Her name was **Djuna Barnes** (1892–1982), and she moved into the house in 1940 and remained there until her death

e.e. cummings's house

forty-two years later. As a reporter for the *Brooklyn Daily Eagle* she had lived and written about the Village since 1915, even writing a few plays for the Provincetown Playhouse. Like so many of her generation, she had lived in Paris until forced home by the events of World War II. While in Paris in 1936, she had written *Nightwood*, her best-known novel, and was quite famous in the bohemian community. As the years went by she became respected as one of the earliest writers in American literature to deal with lesbian relationships. She cut a romantic figure sitting in cafes wearing a black cape, chain-smoking cigarettes, writing, and avoiding contact with as many people as possible. One day when **Carson McCullers**, the author of *The Heart is a Lonely Hunter*, rang her doorbell without an appointment, she was sent away.

Patchin Place, circa 1914

An even more romantic figure lived in Patchin Place before either cummings or Barnes. **John Reed** (1887–1920) moved to New York City to work for *The American Magazine*, and later *The Masses*. He covered stories about labor strife and military actions, and was even arrested for supporting Industrial Workers of the World strikers in the silk mills of New Jersey. In January 1916, he met and fell in love with Louise Bryant, who shared many of his political beliefs, and they rented an apartment together at No. 1 Patchin Place. Reed traveled to Russia just in time to witness the

October Revolution. He was one of the few Americans in Russia during the Revolution, and he covered the story for *The Masses*. He saw the importance of the fall of the Czar and the rise of socialism and began writing his book *Ten Days That Shook The World*, published in 1919. As he grew more sympathetic to the socialist cause, his work came under increased scrutiny in America, and he was charged with sedition. He escaped to Russia using forged papers and died there of typhus in 1920. The Soviet government recognized his contributions to their cause, and he was buried along the wall of the Kremlin, the only American to be so honored. Even though she lived abroad, Louise Bryant continued paying the rent for the apartment on Patchin Place for ten years after his death. She used the apartment to store his manuscripts and notes because she was concerned for their safety. The U.S. Customs Department had confiscated his notes earlier and did not return them for more than a year. Warren Beatty captured Reed's story in the film *Reds* (1980).

And Patchin Place holds still more history. **John Masefield** (1878–1967), England's poet laureate for nearly forty years, lived here before any of the others. As a young man he visited America in 1896 and worked for a while as a busboy at Columbian Gardens, a nearby saloon. The proprietor, Luke O'Connor, took a liking to the young boy and provided him with a small room on Patchin Place, along with his board and ten dollars a month. Masefield, who read Malory's *Morte d'Arthur* while living in an attic room here, decided to return to England and become an author. On later trips to New York, as a famous poet, he always stopped in to see his friend, Luke O'Connor, and talk about old times.

William Brinckley, author of *Don't Go Near the Water*; **Harry Kemp**, known as "The Hobo Poet;" **Padraic Colum**, the wonderful Irish storyteller, and novelist **Jane Bowles** also lived here at one time or another, as did sculptor, Gaston Lachaise. You may enter the courtyard for the gate is always open. Two plaques commemorate cummings's residence here, but nothing exists honoring the others.

Sinclair Lewis's House

37 West 10th Street between Fifth and Sixth Avenues

In August 1928, just after his marriage to journalist **Dorothy Thompson**, **Sinclair Lewis** (1885–1951), moved to 37 West 10th Street. At the time, Lewis was the most famous writer in America. His *Main Street*, which was nominated for a Pulitzer Prize, is a reflection of his affection for small-town life, although he did spend a good deal of his life in New York. Lewis lived off and on in various hotels and apartments in the city while he wrote *Babbitt* and *Arrowsmith*, and he rose in popularity with each new book. He used his large advance for the book *Dodsworth* to buy the house at 37 West 10th, and Dorothy made the house very livable, with casual furniture, an informal and welcoming style, and eight years' worth of accumulated objects from storage. Thompson used the second floor as her office, but life with Lewis, or "Red" as he was known, was not easy. He hated to go out, or to make plans in advance to have friends in, but he loved to do things on the spur of the moment. Lewis frequently came

home with friends and acquaintances who would stay for hours or days on end. When he became tired, he would go upstairs for a nap and tell his visitors not to dare leave until he came back. This was fun for "Red," who rented a hotel room in which to work, but it drove Thompson crazy. She could never work in peace and was always responsible for feeding and entertaining at a moment's notice. Once, after they

Sinclair Lewis

had hosted Frances Perkins at their house, Perkins told friends that Dorothy was much more interesting than her husband.

This was the beginning and the end of the marriage. They stayed at the house on West 10th Street little more than a year, then moved several times to other houses and grew further and further apart. When they finally divorced, Thompson bought a house at 237 East 48th Street in Turtle Bay Gardens, and Lewis moved to a large twenty-ninth floor apartment at 300 Central Park West. Still, there were some bright moments while living on West 10th Street. Lewis received the 1930

Nobel Prize while at this address. When the Swedish representative called to tell him, Lewis thought it was one of his friends with a bad Scandinavian accent making a practical joke and hung up.

Sinclair Lewis's house

Mark Twain's House

14 West 10th Street between Fifth and Sixth Avenues

Mark Twain is truly an American author and belongs as much to New York City as he does to Hannibal, Missouri, where he was raised; San Francisco, where his adventures began; and Hartford, Connecticut, where he lived while writing some of his most famous stories.

Samuel Langhorne Clemens visited New York City frequently starting in 1853 at the age of seventeen, when he worked as a typesetter. Later in life, as the famous author "Mark Twain," he was even nicknamed "The Belle of New York," for he was certainly the cosmopolitan superstar of his era and was wined and dined in the finest places in the city. Twain's first appearance as a lecturer in 1867 was on the stage of the Cooper Union in the East Village, where he gave a humorous account of his travels to the Hawaiian Islands. In that same year he met Olivia Langdon, the future Mrs. Twain, at the St. Nicholas Hotel on Broadway.

Those days were followed by Twain's happiest and most productive periods in which he lived in Connecticut, had three children, and enjoyed tremendous financial and literary success with *The Adventures of Tom Sawyer, Life on the Mississippi,* and *Huckleberry Finn.* Despite large royalties, he invested unwisely. Both a publishing company and the Paige typesetting machine company in which he invested heavily, went bankrupt, and he found himself in serious debt in the 1890s. To alleviate this debt, he stayed in a single room in the Player's Club at 16 Gramercy Park South for almost a year, then toured the world on a five-year lecture circuit that earned him the necessary money to repay his debts and get back on his feet financially. Through all this, his popularity never sagged, and he was welcomed home as a conquering hero.

Upon his return from the tour in 1900, he rented an apartment at 14

West 10th Street where he and his family hosted an endless stream of visitors. His daughter, Clara, remembered that "every day would be like some great festive occasion." Twain's wife became seriously ill, however, and the family moved to the Riverdale section of the Bronx, awaiting her recuperation. She failed to regain her strength and died in 1904, at which point Twain moved back to the same neighborhood, into a house at 21 Fifth Avenue, since torn down. A plaque dedicated to him can be found on the 9th Street side of the Brevoort apartment building at Fifth Avenue and 9th Street.

While living in these New York apartments, Twain began to dress in the familiar white serge suits, in which we always picture him. Visitors to his home often found him laying in his ornately carved Venetian bed, with his head at the foot of the bed so he could enjoy the carving, smoking cigars, and dictating his autobiography to Albert Bigelow Paine. To pass the time, he played pool for hours on end or went for long walks, visiting his favorite clubs like the Lotus, the Metropolitan, the Player's, and the Century. In 1908 he moved to his last residence in Redding, Connecticut, where he died in 1910. He was buried by the Presbyterian Church on Fifth Avenue at 37th Street.

Mark Twain dinner at Delmonico's, northeast corner of Fifth Avenue and 44th Street

Albert Hotel

42 East 11th Street at University Place

Thomas Wolfe (1900–1938) lived in room 2220 at the Albert Hotel, on the corner of University Place and East 10th Street, from 1923 until 1926. The Albert was named for an earlier resident, artist Albert Ryder. It is sometimes difficult to remember how great an influence Thomas Wolfe's books had on the shaping of writing in America during the 1930s. His work, along with that of Hemingway and Fitzgerald, brought a new vitality to pre-World War II literature. Wolfe's novels, like *Look Homeward, Angel*, brought to life the sweeping vision of America from small town to big city. In this book, Eugene Gant traveled from North Carolina to New York to find fame and fortune, just as Wolfe himself did. Wolfe wrote of his love for New York as he approached by train, "The city flashed before me like a glorious jewel, blazing with the thousand rich and brilliant facets of a life so good, so bountiful, so strangely and constantly beautiful and interesting that it seemed intolerable that I should miss a moment of it. I saw the streets swarming with the figures of great men and glorious women." Wolfe was careful to disguise the actual locations that he described in his books. For example, The Albert was called the Hotel Leopold in *Of Time and the River*. Wolfe, like his character Gant, became disillusioned with the "ecstatic Northern city." During his time at The Albert he was lonely and had virtually no friends in the city. Later writers like Jack Kerouac and Lawrence Ferlinghetti would come to the city to retrace Wolfe's footsteps and hope that his influence would rub off on them. Kerouac's first novel, *The Town and the City*, is clearly influenced by Wolfe's work.

Thomas Wolfe came to New York as a fledgling playwright and stayed very briefly in an apartment at 439 West 123rd Street, but had found no producers interested in his plays and was forced to accept a job teaching writing at New York University from 1924 through 1930. The Albert was his first permanent address in the city. While living there, he taught in a classroom in the Brown Building at the corner of Washington Place and Greene Street. After the publication of *Look Homeward, Angel* in 1929, however, it seemed that his success was assured, and he quit teaching in order to write full time. Wolfe had several apartments in this part of the city and moved frequently. From his apartment at The Albert he moved on to live in a $35-per-month loft at 13 East 8th Street with the designer Aline Bernstein in late 1926. She became his mistress and exerted a strong influence on his life and work. It was there that he prepared the final version of *Look Homeward, Angel* with his editor, Maxwell Perkins. That building no longer stands. In 1927 he moved to 263 West 11th Street and in 1928, to 27 West 15th Street. He finally wound up at the Chelsea Hotel in 1937, where his last two novels, *Of Time and the River* and *You Can't Go Home Again*, were put together from earlier writings;

Hotel Albert

they were published after his death in 1938. His apartments were always unkempt and cluttered with manuscripts and dirty clothes. His later years were marked by extreme alcoholism, contributing to his early death while traveling in Baltimore.

Strand Bookstore

828 Broadway at East 12th Street

In New York, where specialization is the rule, neighborhoods attracted one type of business or another. There was a diamond district, a fur district, a wedding gown district, and once upon a time, a used-book district on Fourth Avenue between 14th Street and Astor Place. During the late nineteenth and most of the last century, as many as twenty-two stores operated at any one time along a four-block stretch with books displayed outdoors in bins. In 1949, **Jack Kerouac** used some of his first book advance check on Fourth Avenue to buy a collection of classics. Instead, as he wrote to Alfred Kazin, "I wound up being depressed at the sight of vast piles of useless and meaningless dusty literature ..." Hollywood gave a romantic glimpse into one of the stores in the movie *Funny Face*, where Fred Astaire discovered Audrey Hepburn working as a bohemian sales clerk and whisked her away to Paris. Now, almost every vestige of "Book Row" is gone.

One exception is the Strand Bookstore, known as "The Strand." It is the largest bookstore in the country, and as their advertising states, they house over "8 Miles of Books." It has nearly two million volumes. However you do the math, The Strand has a lot of books,

Strand Bookstore

crammed into every available nook and cranny on four floors of the building at the corner of Broadway and East 12th Street. Books even spill out into the bargain bins lining the outside of the store, just as they once did on old Book Row. This old-fashioned bookstore "will never serve cappuccino!" the owner Fred Bass proudly states in every interview. Since his father founded the store in 1927 on Book Row, The Strand has been recycling books, buying and selling trash and treasures alike. Umberto Eco calls this his "favorite place in America" and it's not unlikely that every writer in New York gets to the Strand at one time or another. Steven Spielberg even ordered an entire library of 30,000 titles from The Strand. (Whether he read them all or not is another matter.)

Jack Kerouac, 1957

Jewish Daily Forward Building

173–175 East Broadway between Rutgers and Jefferson Streets

At one time this block of East Broadway on the Lower East Side was known as the "Publishers Row" of Yiddish newspapers. The *Jewish Daily Forward* at 173–175 East Broadway was the most important of five newspapers that were published here. *The Jewish Daily Forward* or *Forverts* was founded in 1897 during a time when the influx of Yiddish-speaking immigrants into New York City was at its highest level. Under the editorship of **Abraham Cahan** from 1903 to 1951, the *Forward* quickly became one of the leading newspapers in the city and reached a peak circulation of over 200,000 during the 1920s, the largest Yiddish daily newspaper in the world. Since its early days, the audience for Yiddish newspapers has dropped steadily, and in 1990, the *Forward* began weekly publication and an English-language edition. The twelve-story building was erected in 1911–12 by architect George A. Boehm and housed many Jewish social and benevolent organizations besides the *Forward*. Today the offices of the *Forward* have been moved to 45 East 33rd Street and this building is currently under major renovation. The exterior of the building has been declared a landmark and retains the "Forward Building" name and ornamentation.

The *Forward* published literature as well as news items. *The Forward*'s most popular column, called "Bintel Brief," or "Bundle of Letters," was a forerunner of the "Dear Abby"-style advice columns that are still popular in newspapers today. Immigrants wrote questions about adapting to American culture, and the editors answered them, often provoking heated discussions on a variety of topics. Long before the writer **Sholom Aleichem** moved to America in 1905, he sent stories for publication in the *Forward*. Aleichem, a pseudonym of **Solomon Rabinowitz**, wrote novels and short stories based on the lives of poor Russian Jews under the Czars. One of his stories, "Tevye's Daughters," was turned into the Broadway musical, *Fiddler on the Roof*. Once settled in America, Aleichem continued to write for the *Forward* until his death in 1916.

The most famous writer connected with the *Forward* was **Isaac Bashevis Singer**. Escaping the persecution of Jews in Poland in 1933, Isaac's brother and fellow-writer Israel Joshua Singer, settled in New York City. He invited his brother to follow him to America in 1935. Israel found Isaac a job on the staff of the *Forward*, where Isaac worked for the next forty years. He began writing book reviews and human interest stories, and later developed the storytelling style for which he

Issac Bashevis Singer

won the Nobel Prize in Literature in 1978. Singer lived all his life on New York's Upper West Side, and traveled by subway to his office to work. He wrote exclusively in Yiddish, and the readers of the *Forward* eagerly awaited his stories. Only after their initial Yiddish publication were his stories translated into English. Beginning with the publication of his story, "Gimpel the Fool," which Saul Bellow translated into English in 1953, Singer began to enjoy a wider popularity. A favorite restaurant of Singer's was the Garden Cafeteria at 165 East Broadway and Rutgers Street, where intellectuals could sit for hours and talk over the events of the day. Leon Trotsky and Fidel Castro also ate in the Garden, but like the *Forward* building, the restaurant has been swallowed up by Chinatown's growth and is now the Wing Shoon Restaurant.

Allen Ginsberg's Apartment
170 East 2nd Street between Avenues A and B

Allen Ginsberg, one of the most talented and influential poets of the twentieth century, lived for most of his life in New York City. Although born and raised in nearby Paterson, New Jersey, he attended Columbia University and maintained apartments in the East Village from that time until his death at the age of seventy. In 1956 he published *Howl and Other Poems,* which was seized by customs officials; he was charged with obscenity. The ensuing trial made the poem a cause célèbre, and the court decided that a work could not be banned if it had "redeeming social value." The publication of "Howl" sparked public interest in a group of writers that would come to be known as the Beat Generation. Other important members of the group were **Jack Kerouac, William S. Burroughs, Gregory Corso,** and **Lawrence Ferlinghetti**, all of whom lived in New York City at one time or another. Ginsberg himself was portrayed by Kerouac in many of his books, such as *On the Road* and *The Dharma Bums.*

From August 1958 until March 1961, Ginsberg and his lifelong companion, Peter Orlovsky, lived in apartment 16 of "The Croton" at 170 East 2nd Street. While living here Ginsberg wrote most of "Kaddish," widely considered to be his greatest poem. The poem is a lament for his crazy dead mother and begins with the line "Strange now to think of you, gone without corsets & eyes, while I walk on the sunny pavement of Greenwich Village." Ginsberg was visited in the apartment by writer friends such as Gregory Corso, **Herbert Huncke, Bob Kaufman,** Jack Kerouac, **Norman Mailer, Alex Trocchi,** and **Lew Welch. Timothy Leary** came on weekends from his teaching job at Harvard, and here they began to plan the psychedelic revolution of the 1960s. Ginsberg's resi-

Allen Ginsberg, 1953

dence was recently commemorated with a plaque near the door of the apartment house. Ginsberg also lived in several other apartments in the neighborhood, including his final one at 404 East 14th Street where he died from cancer in 1997. By that time he had won a National Book Award for poetry and been elected into the respected American Academy of Arts and Letters.

Nuyorican Poets Cafe

236 East 3rd Street between Avenues B and C

The Nuyorican Poets Cafe was originally located at 505 East 6th Street before it moved to 236 East 3rd Street in 1980. Founded in 1974 as an outgrowth of a salon hosted since 1972 by **Miguel Algarin** and **Richard August**, the idea was to provide a place for meetings and performances of special interest to the Spanish-speaking community of the Lower East Side. Its name is a combination of the words New York and Puerto Rican. The Nuyorican attracted writers such as **Lucky Cienfuegos, Miguel Piñero, Pedro Pietri, Tato Laviera, Bimbo Rivas, Sandra Maria Esteves**, and **Piri Thomas.** Although originally intended to provide a forum for the Latino community, the cafe soon attracted other East Village figures such as **Amiri Baraka, Gregory Corso, Allen Ginsberg, and Ntozake Shange**. New writers emerged through from its open readings including **Paul Beatty, Maggie Estep, Reggie Gaines, David Henderson, Jimmy**

The Nuyorican Poets Cafe

Santiago Baca, Sapphire, and Edwin Torres.

Gregory Corso and Allen Ginsberg, 1952

Works like Piñero's *Short Eyes* (1974) and Pietri's *Puerto Rican Obituary* (1974) were written and revised at the Nuyorican Cafe. The cafe closed between 1983 and 1989, but reopened in the same location on East 3rd Street. Since then it has sponsored weekly readings and poetry slams, sometimes hosted by Bob Holman. The monthly program of screenplay readings has revealed many new, creative voices to producers and directors in the city. In 1994, an anthology, *Aloud: Voices from the Nuyorican Poets Cafe,* was published.

The Nuyorican is a drafty, bare-brick space that serves as meeting room, dance hall, auditorium, and café. People come here for the adventure of hearing something new and discovering something fresh, not for the luxury of the surroundings. Especially exciting are poetry slams, when the poets read work that is judged and scored like an athletic event. A very small prize is given to the winner, but as the emcee states, "The best poet always loses." A schedule of events can be found at the Nuyorican's box office or in the poetry calendars in weekly magazines and newspapers.

McSorley's Old Ale House

15 East 7th Street between Second and Third Avenues

When McSorley's opened its doors for business in 1854, Franklin Pierce was President, the Civil War was still a decade away, and lunch was free to patrons. The assortment of customers was motley then, just as it is today. Truck drivers, police officers, politicians, artists, and writers are attracted to McSorley's because it never changes. The only significant change happened in 1970 when McSorley's was forced by the courts to admit women. After that, the motto was amended from "Good Ale, Raw Onions, and No Ladies" to "Good Ale and Raw Onions." McSorley's, in every other way, has not changed. When pictures were put on the walls in the 1800s they stayed there, even as other items were added in the intervening years. The souvenirs helped draw tourists and visitors to McSorley's even more than the ale and onions with saltine crackers. On permanent display, you will find everything from theater and sports memorabilia to the chair of Peter Cooper, the founder of nearby Cooper Union, a mug that Cooper engraved with an ice pick, and flags, cartoons, clippings, and photographs.

Four Presidents, including Lincoln and Clinton, have stopped in for a drink at the bar, and writers and artists have found it especially relaxing to wile away the hours next to the potbelly stove on cold winter days. Irish writer **Brendan Behan** was a regular when he was in town and his favorite spot was a corner seat near the fire. One day Behan had a fight with the owner because he had called him a "FBI man." After the tavern owner explained that FBI stood for "Foreign-Born Irish," Behan saw the joke and they became friends again. John Sloan painted pictures of the bar at least four times and one of the paintings is in the

Whitney Museum's permanent collection. His friends, George Luks, Glenn O. Coleman, and Stuart Davis also painted the place.

McSorley's Old Ale House

New Yorker columnist **Joseph Mitchell** wrote a famous article about McSorley's in 1940 called "The Old House at Home."

e.e. cummings wrote a poem about McSorley's Saloon, which begins:

"i was sitting in mcsorley's. outside it was New York

and beautifully snowing. inside snug and evil . . ."

Beat poets **Paul Blackburn** and **LeRoi Jones** (now **Amiri Baraka**) were also regulars. And you can be sure that **Allen Ginsberg** and **Jack Kerouac** stopped in on their way to hear jazz at the Five Spot just around the corner. Diverse writers such as poet and novelist **Gilbert Sorrentino** and **H. L. Mencken**'s fellow editor, **George Jean Nathan**, were commonly seen at the tables. Today's luminaries include **Malachi** and **Frank McCourt**, who have been known to have a mug or two here on occasion. Even the current bartender, Geoffrey Bartholomew, is publishing a book of his own poems about McSorley's.

Ale is sold by the pair, and there is only one choice, light or dark—no mixed drinks here. Regulars will point out their favorite items to you if you ask, whether it's the Civil War–era wishbones above the bar, the copy of Lincoln's saloon license, the photo of Babe Ruth, or Houdini's handcuffs, permanently attached to the bar rail at the floor.

W. H. Auden's Apartment

77 St. Mark's Place between First and Second Avenues

A plaque no longer marks the home of **W. H. Auden** as it once did at 77 St. Mark's Place, where the poet lived from 1953 until 1972. During a recent renovation the bronze tablet was removed and never replaced, one of the many literary mysteries of New York City. Wystan Hugh Auden was born in England in 1907 and educated at Oxford, where he took up poetry after exploring many other disciplines. His classmates included several future literary figures such as **Louis MacNeice**, **Cecil Day Lewis** (father of Daniel Day Lewis) and **Stephen Spender**. Immediately after graduation Auden began extensive travels and a one-year stay in Berlin with his friend Christopher Isherwood. Their adventures in Germany between the wars is retold in Isherwood's *Berlin Stories*, one of which was transformed into the Broadway musical *Cabaret*.

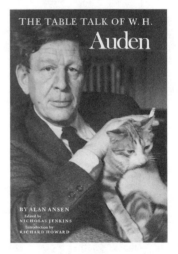

THE TABLE TALK OF W. H. Auden

BY ALAN ANSEN
Edited by
NICHOLAS JENKINS
Introduction by
RICHARD HOWARD

Auden's own literary fame grew with the publication of several books and collaborations during the 1930s. In 1939, he and Isherwood sailed for America, where Auden lived for the rest of his life. Although Auden loved England, he wanted to escape from what he considered the inbred, stultifying literary world of London. His fellow countrymen believed that he was abandoning his homeland just on the brink of World War II and many considered him a traitor. A few months after his arrival in the

United States he met **Chester Kallman**, who, after a brief romantic relationship, became his lifelong friend and collaborator. During these early years, Auden wrote some of his greatest poetry. It is collected in *Another Time*, published in 1940, and *The Age of Anxiety*, published in 1948, for which he received the Pulitzer Prize.

After living in various places around the country, Auden settled into an apartment at 77 St. Mark's Place in 1953. For most of the following nineteen years that Auden lived here, he shared his apartment with Kallman. It was a floor-through apartment with a sleeping room off the living room, a separate study for Auden, and a large, cluttered kitchen where they had gourmet meals and memorable dinner parties. Besides his old friends Isherwood and Stephen Spender, people such as Igor Stravinsky and Allen Ginsberg often visited to pay their respects to one of the greatest poets of the twentieth century. Someone reported the apartment as "a sad scene of sagging bookshelves, sprung-seat overstuffed chairs, a dusty and scarred 'cozy-corner' and everywhere litter, piles of paper and magazines, this morning's crusted dish of egg." Amid the clutter one visitor also spotted a hungry mouse feeding on the unwashed dishes and decided not to stay for dinner.

Ignoring the fact that Auden was gay, one woman stalked him for years while he was living here. Once, she bribed the superintendent of the building to let her into his apartment, where she measured his suit and bought him a new one. She told people she was pregnant by Auden, although they had met only once—at a hearing when she was committed to a psychiatric ward. Auden wrote *City Without Walls* and *Epistle to a Godson* at 77 St. Mark's Place. He wrote the libretto for *Elegy for Young Lovers* in 1959 with Chester Kallman. He became a regular fixture in the neighborhood, and attended St. Mark's Episcopal Church just around the corner. When he died, the newspaper sent a reporter to interview the dry cleaner, grocery and hardware store clerks, who all knew him well. His poetry continues to be popular, one poem even finding its way into the recent movie, *Four Weddings and a Funeral*.

Poetry Project at
St. Mark's Church

Second Avenue and East 10th Street

St. Mark's-in-the-Bowery is an Episcopal church at the corner of East 10th Street and Second Avenue. It was originally the family chapel of the Stuyvesant family, and Peter Stuyvesant, the old Dutch governor, is buried in the churchyard. The church is the second oldest in the city, built in 1799; the steeple was added in 1828. Twice, the church has been severely damaged by fire, most recently in the late 1970s, but it has been carefully restored each time. This church's liberal attitude towards artists began long ago. In the first half of the century, **Isadora Duncan**, **Carl Sandburg**, **Kahlil Gibran**, **Harry Houdini**, **Frank Lloyd Wright**, and **William Carlos Williams** spoke or performed here.

St. Mark's is now the home of the Poetry Project, one of the most vital and long-lived groups of writers in the city. In the mid-1960s, poet **Paul Blackburn** helped set up poetry readings here after the closing of the Café Le Metro down the street. For decades, there had been a tradition in the East Village of weeknight poetry readings, usually in a coffee-house or bar, but this was the first time that they assembled in a church. The success they enjoyed led them to establish the St. Mark's Poetry Project. Joel Oppenheimer was the first director and Anne Waldman his assistant; she took over as director after he left. So many poets and writers of the New York School, Black Mountain, and Beat Generation groups have read here in the past thirty years, it would take a small book just to list them all. Some of the writers who have read here include: **John Ashbery**, **Amiri Baraka**, **Charles Bukowski**, **William S. Burroughs**, **Gregory Corso**, **Diane di Prima**, **Bob Dylan**, **Lawrence Fer-**

linghetti, Allen Ginsberg, Kenneth Koch, Denise Levertov, Robert Lowell, James Merrill, James Schuyler, Gary Snyder, and **Philip Whalen.**

For decades the church provided a mimeograph machine for the poets to use, and scores of influential little magazines were published here as well as the Poetry Project's own magazine, *The World*. Each year on New Year's Day, a mammoth poetry marathon is held as a fund-raiser for the Poetry Project, with many celebrity readers contributing their time. Yoko Ono, Patti Smith, Lou Reed, Sam Shepard, and Robert Wilson have all participated in years past.

Of related interest is "Poet's Grove," a name given by writer **Edward Sanders** to the group of trees dedicated to deceased Poetry Project members. There are plaques near the side entrance to the parish hall identifying trees planted for W. H. Auden, Paul Blackburn, Ted Berrigan, Allen Ginsberg, Frank O'Hara, and Michael Scholnick.

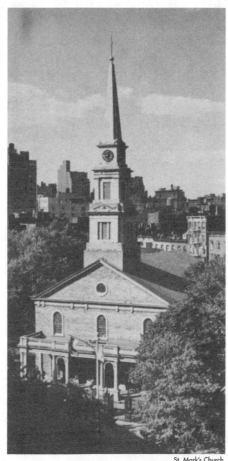

St. Mark's Church

77

Jack Kerouac's Apartment

454 West 20th Street between Ninth and Tenth Avenues

The apartment building where **Jack Kerouac** wrote his most famous novel, *On the Road*, is at 454 West 20th Street, between Ninth and Tenth Avenues. In the mid-1940s, Jack Kerouac, **William S. Burroughs**, and **Allen Ginsberg** formed the nucleus of the literary movement now known as the Beat Generation. Kerouac spent most of his life either "on the road" or living in his mother's house. Although strongly identified with New York City, he never had his own apartment in the city. The apartment he shared here in 1951 with his second wife, **Joan Haverty**, was rented in her name.

After living with Kerouac's mother for a few months just after their marriage, Joan Haverty decided to move. She knew there was no way the marriage could last if they continued to live under the same roof with Jack's domineering mother. In January 1951, she rented an apartment in this four-story, red-brick row house, and a few days later, Jack agreed to move in with her. Here, Kerouac stumbled upon the idea of typing on a long roll of paper so that his thoughts could flow without stopping for paper changes. He wrote his books so quickly that Truman Capote cruelly quipped, "That isn't writing, it's typing." In the three weeks between April 2 and April 22, 1951, he used strips of art paper taped together to write *On the Road*. Most of the best-selling novel was typed at this apartment; the rest at a friend's loft nearby.

A week after the Kerouacs moved in, **Neal Cassady** arrived in New York City from Denver. He was Kerouac's model for Dean Moriarity, the legendary Western Adonis, who epitomized the restless, free-spirited individualism of post-war America in the novel. In the final scene of

On the Road, Dean Moriarity (Cassady) and Sal Paradise (Jack Kerouac) say good-bye to each other in front of this apartment and go their separate ways. Before long, Jack and Joan went their separate ways as well. In June, when she told him she might be pregnant, he suggested she have an abortion. Kerouac never acknowledged that her daughter was his, and he returned to live with his mother for the rest of his short life. He died of alcoholism in 1969, at the age of forty-seven.

Jack Kerouac, 1953

Hotel Chelsea

222 West 23rd Street between Seventh and Eighth Avenues

In Chelsea, one literary landmark stands out among all the others, the Hotel Chelsea at 222 West 23rd Street between Seventh and Eighth Avenues. "The Chelsea" has more creative names associated with it than any other building in the city. Designed in 1884 by Hubert, Pirsson and Company, it was one of New York's first cooperative apartment buildings. The large Victorian Gothic building is distinguished by its delicate wrought iron balconies and massive brick facade. In 1905 it became a hotel, although long-term residents have always made up the majority of its tenants.

From the start, the Chelsea hosted literary lights such as **William Dean Howells**, literary critic and the author of *The Rise of Silas Lapham*, and **Mark Twain**, who stayed at

Hotel Chelsea

the hotel while on tour in 1888. Melville Dewey, the founder of Columbia's School of Library Science and inventor of the Dewey Decimal System, lived here at the same time. **William Sydney Porter**, better known as **O. Henry**, kept a room on West 26th Street for writing, but actually lived in a suite at the hotel in the early 1900s when he was working on his popular short stories.

In the 1930s, **Edgar Lee Masters** moved into the hotel and wrote a poem about its history, asking:

> *Who will remember that Mark Twain used to stroll*
> *In the gorgeous dining room, that Princesses,*
> *Poets and celebrated actresses*
> *Lived here and made its soul . . .*

It was through Masters that **Thomas Wolfe** came to the hotel in 1937 with a trunk full of manuscripts that included *The Web and the Rock* and *You Can't Go Home Again.* These he assembled in his eighth-floor suite in the months before his death. They were published posthumously, after his sudden death in Baltimore in September 1938 at the age of thirty-seven.

Thomas Wolfe

In the fifties, writers such as **James T. Farrell**, who wrote the Studs Lonigan trilogy, **Mary McCarthy**, and the more flamboyant **Dylan Thomas** stayed at the Chelsea. On a night in November 1953, while on his fourth reading tour of America, Thomas fell into an alcohol-induced coma when he returned to the hotel from the White Horse Tavern. He was rushed to nearby St. Vincent's Hospital where he died. His poems, "Do Not Go Gentle Into That Good Night," and "A Child's Christmas in Wales," remain among the most popular in the English language.

Another hard-drinking writer, **Brendan Behan**, also stayed at the Hotel Chelsea. In 1961, he was accused of chasing the maids at the more staid

Algonquin Hotel uptown and asked to leave. In his book, *Brendan Behan's New York*, he asked the proprietor of the Chelsea to leave space on the memorial plaques at the front door for his name. He passed away only a few years later in 1964 and his name was indeed added. **Arthur Miller**, author of *Death of a Salesman*, lived here at the same time. He loved the hotel and considered this the only hotel in the city without class distinctions.

In the 1970s, the hotel continued to make literary news, for it was here that **Clifford Irving** lived when arrested for writing his fake autobiography of millionaire recluse, Howard Hughes. Other guests may not have been as notorious but still made notable contributions to literature.

William S. Burroughs, 1953

Arthur C. Clarke wrote the book *2001: A Space Odyssey* while in residence, and **Nelson Algren**, **Robert Flaherty**, **Julius Lester**, **Vladimir Nabokov**, and **Yevgeny Yevtushenko** all stayed at the Chelsea.

More recently the hotel has been the home of yet another wave of the counter-culture. **William S. Burroughs**, author of *Naked Lunch*, lived here as did fellow Beats such as poet **Gregory Corso**, storyteller Herbert Huncke, and filmmaker Harry Smith. **James Schuyler** lived here for many years, writing poems that appeared in his Pulitzer Prize–winning book *Morning of the Poem*. He died in 1991. **Lawrence Ferlinghetti**, **Gary Snyder**, **Andrei Voznesensky**, and **Philip Whalen** also stayed here when in town.

Each decade brings a new group to the hotel, and it isn't limited to literary figures, either. Sarah Bernhardt and Lillian Russell lived here in the nineteenth century, and since then, John Sloan painted here, Virgil Thomson composed here for fifty years, Andy Warhol made a movie here, and punk-rock star Patti Smith lived here with photographer Robert Mapplethorpe. Bob Dylan wrote his "Sad-Eyed Lady of the Lowlands" here, and Jimi Hendrix, Janis Joplin, The Grateful Dead, The Mamas and Papas, and The Jefferson Airplane all roomed here. But the most publicized and infamous event to take place at the Hotel Chelsea was the 1978 murder, in Room 100, of Nancy Spungen by her boyfriend, Sid Vicious, of the Sex Pistols. He took his own life before the trial.

The elegance of the original hotel has disappeared. The original dining room where Thomas Wolfe ate has been turned into a Spanish restaurant. The grand staircase has been blocked off for fire safety regulations, and the ornate furnishings and decorated ceilings are gone. But the lobby still boasts an interesting collection of art donated in lieu of tenant's rent, including work by Larry Rivers, André François, Patrick Hughes, and other New York School artists. An exciting new bar, Serena, just opened in the hotel's basement. Take time to read the brass memorials outside the entrance, a Who's Who of New York's literary past, and drink in the atmosphere that still pervades the lobby.

Washington Irving Statue
Irving Place at East 17th Street

When developer Samuel B. Ruggles designed Gramercy Park and the surrounding area in 1831, he named the street to the south of the park Irving Place in honor of **Washington Irving** (1783–1859). Irving was one of the most popular writers in nineteenth-century America, and Ruggles hoped that Gramercy Park, at that time a remote location, would become just as popular. Within a short time, Gramercy Park became one of New York's most exclusive addresses.

This is not the only association with Irving in the neighborhood, though. In 1885 sculptor Friedrich Beer cast a colossal bronze bust of the author to be placed in Central Park. Before that could happen, the Park Commissioners had to get the approval of the Art Committee. In their opinion, Beer had not been able to capture the dignity of Washington Irving, and they turned down the request. As a result, the monument was placed in Bryant Park for the next fifty years. In 1935, the bust was relocated to the front of Washington Irving High School at the corner of Irving Place and East 17th Street, where it has stood ever since.

Washington Irving was born in lower Manhattan, at 111 William Street, in a house long since demolished. Early on he showed an interest in literature, and even though he passed his

Washington Irving

bar examinations, he turned instead to writing. In 1807, he and two of his brothers began a magazine, which poked fun at the town's foibles. They called the magazine *Salmagundi* after the spicy stew of meat, herring, and onions. Today the Salmagundi Club at 47 Fifth Avenue carries on this name. Irving was also the first writer to use the name Gotham to describe New York City, a name that has stuck ever since. Gotham was a cunning sixteenth-century English village that avoided being heavily taxed when every citizen pretended to be crazy.

Irving also wrote a series of stories under the pseudonym Diedrich Knickerbocker called *A History of New York, from the Beginning of the World to the End of the Dutch Dynasty,* which described both fictional and non-fictional events from New York's past. (Anyone familiar with New York sports knows that the basketball team is named the "Knicks," after Irving's pen name.) These works were tremendously popular throughout the country, and Irving became the first American to earn a living solely through his writings. His characters Rip Van Winkle and Ichabod Crane are still well-known today. In 1832 he returned to New York, after seventeen years in Europe, and lived on Colonnade Row at 434 Lafayette Street near Astor Place.

The neighborhood along Irving Place has long been considered Irving territory, due in part to a misleading memorial. Across the street from the school at 122 East 17th Street, is an ancient building that overlooks the statue of Irving. On the 17th Street side of the building is an elaborate plaque stating that Washington Irving lived there, but in fact he did not. Whether it was placed there by error due to the fact that a man named Edgar Irving had lived there during Washington's lifetime, or by the wishful thinking of an earlier admirer of Irving, is not known. One person who did live in the house was Elizabeth Marbury, a literary agent who represented both Oscar Wilde and George Bernard Shaw. It is likely that Wilde would have visited her at this address on his New York lecture tour in 1883, as he stayed in rooms next door at No. 47 Irving Place.

Pete's Tavern

66 Irving Place at East 18th Street

One of the oldest saloons in the city, with what is certainly one of the most beautiful bars, Pete's Tavern is located at the corner of Irving Place and East 18th Street. It opened in 1864 as a tavern with rooms to rent upstairs and stables for horses out back. It has never closed, even during Prohibition when it remained open as a speakeasy serving the politicos from nearby Tammany Hall. (The front was converted into a make-believe florist shop with a door opening into the speakeasy through a fake refrigerator.) This location, in a building built in 1829, served as a grocery as early as 1852 and since "groceries" occasionally sold ale at the counter, there is a controversy as to whether Pete's shouldn't be given credit for being the oldest bar in New York City. McSorley's, which was opened in 1854, is considered the oldest in continuous operation.

Pete's Tavern

Pete's is most often associated with **O. Henry**, its favorite son, who lived from 1903 until 1906 nearby at 55 Irving Place. O. Henry is a very interesting character himself. Born in 1862 as **William Sydney Porter**, he had already spent several years in the Ohio State Penitentiary for embezzlement before coming to New York City in 1902, where he began to write the short stories that made him famous. He did not live long enough to enjoy his fame. He died in 1910 in New York, but his books like *The Four Million* and *The Voice of the City* live on. The Friends of the Library Association placed a plaque on the front of Pete's in 1999 to honor O. Henry and **Ludwig Bemelmans**, who also hung out here while creating his adorable heroine, *Madeline*.

In O. Henry's day, Pete's Tavern was called Healy's Cafe and was one of the places he liked to sit and watch the world go by, making up stories about the people he'd see in the neighborhood. It is thought that one of these stories, "The Gift of the Magi," was written while he was sitting at the second booth inside the door in 1905, and a plaque on the booth commemorates this. Scholars have debated the point, and it is believed that if it wasn't written here, at least the inspiration was born here and the story written back in his apartment. His story, "The Lost Blend," was definitely inspired by Pete's, for that was the name of his favorite alcoholic concoction served at the bar. A plaque next to the doorway of Sal Anthony's restaurant at 55 Irving Place commemorates O. Henry's residence.

Enjoy a leisurely lunch or an afternoon break from touring the literary landmarks of New York at Pete's. Maybe you'll write a short story of your own. You'll also understand why the bar has been used for the filming of several movies such as *Ragtime* and countless television commercials— it's the very image of an old-time New York bar, with beveled glass mirrors and dark wood carvings everywhere. When you leave Pete's, walk over to No. 55 Irving Place to read another plaque there that claims "The Gift of the Magi" was written in that house in "two feverish hours."

National Arts Club and Players Club

15-16 Gramercy Park South

Gramercy Park is an especially beautiful part of New York City. On the south side of the park, there are two clubs steeped in literary tradition.

The Players at No. 16 is a private club founded in 1888 by and for men interested in theater, music, literature, and the arts. One of the founders, Edwin Booth, was the greatest Shakespearean actor in America. Booth bought the 1845 Gothic Revival brownstone facing the park in 1888 and asked his close friend Stanford White to remodel it as a club. White agreed and asked for a lifetime membership in the club in lieu of a fee. Inside is the Hampden-Booth Theatre Library, which contains Booth's own library of theatrical history as well as his diaries, notes, and prompt-books. Booth died in his own room here in 1893, and that room has been lovingly preserved intact on the third floor. Literary members included **Vachel Lindsay**, **Edgar Lee Masters**, **Thomas Nast**, **Booth Tarkington**, and **Mark Twain**. Peer through the gates at Booth's statue by Edmond T. Quinn across the street in the center of the park, dedicated in 1918. Booth is dressed in the costume of Hamlet, his greatest role, rising from a chair to make his famous soliloquy. Unfortunately, the sidewalk outside the park is as close as you'll get—Gramercy Park is the last private park in Manhattan and only the residents of the surrounding buildings have keys.

Next door at No. 15 is the National Arts Club. This building from the 1840s, also Gothic Revival in style, was remodeled in 1884. Calvert Vaux, famous for his work on Central Park with Frederick Law Olmstead, was the architect, and he worked out a design inspired by John Ruskin, using various colors of stones with medallions of **Dante, Goethe, Milton,** and others to adorn the facade. The club originally was built as a home

National Arts Club and Players Club Exterior, c. 1895

for Samuel J. Tilden, who ran for President against Rutherford B. Hayes in 1876. Until the Bush-Gore election, he was the only candidate to win the popular vote and lose in the electoral college voting. His extensive personal library and fortune provided the basis for the New York Public Library, founded in 1895. In 1906, the

National Arts Club took over the Tilden mansion. Unlike their neighbors at The Players, the National Arts Club did not restrict female members. Anna Hyatt Huntington was an early member and her interests, like those

National Arts Club and Players Club Interior, c. 1895

of the entire membership of the National Arts Club, were in art and literature. Members included Henry Clay Frick, J. P. Morgan, Teddy Roosevelt, and Woodrow Wilson, as well as most of the era's great artists and illustrators, such as Augustus Saint-Gaudens, William Merritt Chase, and Frederick Remington. Literary

members have included W. H. Auden, Padraic Colum, Hamlin Garland, editor Richard Watson Gilder and Robert Cortes Holliday. Holliday, besides being a subject for books by Booth Tarkington, was also the editor and literary executor for Joyce Kilmer, the author of the poem "Trees."

Herman Melville's Last Home

104 East 26th Street between Park Avenue South and Lexington Avenue

One of nineteenth-century America's greatest writers, **Herman Melville**, was born in New York City, lived in New York much of his life, and died here in obscurity. He was born in 1819 at 6 Pearl Street in lower Manhattan. His birthplace no longer exists and has been replaced by a modern office building. Melville's father was an importer of French fabrics and his mother was a member of the prominent Dutch Gansevoort family, after whom several streets and structures in the city were named. While still a young man, his father's business went bankrupt, and the younger Melville was forced to take a wide

Site of Herman Melville's house

variety of jobs to earn his keep, including banking, farming, and teaching. For several years he worked as a sailor, and his experiences on the high seas gave him the inspiration for many of his books. On his second voyage, his captain was so cruel that Melville jumped ship in the Marquesas Islands, lived with cannibals for several months, and joined the crew of another ship for the return voyage to America.

Upon his return, in 1844, he began to write a book based on his adventures and sea travels, calling it *Typee*, after the name of the cannibal tribe. This was received with enthusiasm by the public, and it was quickly followed by *Omoo, Mardi, Redburn,* and *White Jacket*. In 1851, he published his masterpiece, *Moby Dick*, a further account of the harsh lives of sailors, this time in search of the white whale with the obsessed Captain Ahab as their leader. Readers did not understand the symbolism in *Moby Dick* and it was not a success. It was treated with such a degree of non-importance that when his next book, *Pierre,* was published to bad reviews, Melville decided to give up writing as a career, although he continued to write in his spare time.

Shortly after these disappointments Melville took a job as a customs inspector at the docks in the West Village and remained there for thirty years. He retired to a quiet life, continuing to write stories like *Billy Budd* that would not be published in his lifetime. He died without notice in 1891 in his home at 104 East 26th Street, where he had lived since 1863. His obituary identified him as "Herman Melville, formerly a well-known author." Though the house is gone, a plaque remains on the 26th Street side of the building at 357 Park Avenue South. It wasn't until the 1920s that scholars began to take notice of his writings again, and realized that *Moby Dick* is perhaps the greatest American novel ever written.

Pierpont Morgan Library

29 East 36th Street

John Pierpont Morgan (1837–1913), one of the richest men in the world, was also one of the greatest book collectors of all time. Aside from business and book collecting, Morgan's major interests were in art. He lived in a mansion on the corner of East 36th Street and Madison Avenue. In order to house his collection of books and manuscripts he purchased all the property on the north side of the street next to his house and asked Charles McKim, of the firm McKim, Mead and White, to design a library. The result was the beautiful Morgan Library, which was completed in 1906 at the cost of more than $1.2 million, quite a sizeable amount at the time. After Morgan's death, his collection was opened to the public. His mansion was torn down and in 1928 a new museum building was added at the corner. More recently his son's house at the corner of East 37th Street was added to the museum complex, with a courtyard restaurant connecting the buildings. It is a nice, relaxing place to stop for a weekend brunch or afternoon tea.

The interior of the marble Italian Renaissance palazzo is divided into several parts. A large area is devoted to changing exhibitions, but Morgan's own private study is maintained just as it was on the day he died. His wealth is reflected in the subtle opulence of the room. Morgan's favorite paintings by Cranach the Elder, Memling, Cima da Conegliano and other

Pierpont Morgan Library

European artists hang on the walls. Across the hallway is the original library lined with shelves on three levels containing the treasures he collected. Throughout the building, special attention has been paid to the details of design. Library and printer's devices are carved into the ceilings, murals represent classical literary themes, and friezes symbolize tragic and lyric poetry.

Sir Kenneth Clark aptly described the Morgan Library with these words: "There are larger collections in the capitals of Europe, but in the Morgan one feels that every object is a treasure, every item is perfect." Included among those treasures are three copies of the Gutenberg Bible, one of which is always on view. The collection of medieval and Renais-

East rooms of Morgan Library

sance manuscripts is outstanding in its scope, and it is supported by an enormous collection of drawings and prints. Of special note are the ninth-century Lindau Gospels, the tenth-century Beatus, the Book of Hours of Catherine of Cleves, and the Book of Hours of Cardinal Alessandro Farnese, the most famous Italian Renaissance manuscript in the world.

Morgan was also interested in manuscripts by major literary and historical figures. The highlights include the original manuscript for Charles Dickens's *A Christmas Carol*, Henry David Thoreau's journals, and Thomas Jefferson's letters to his daughter. There are also important materials from Jane Austen, Charlotte Brontë, Lord Byron, Albert Einstein, John Keats, Abraham Lincoln, John Milton, John Steinbeck, and Voltaire, to name only a few. Morgan was also interested in collecting music manuscripts, and his collection includes original works by Bach, Beethoven, Brahms, Gilbert and Sullivan, Mozart, Schubert, and Stravinsky.

New York Public Library

Fifth Avenue at 42nd Street

Entire books have been written about the main research branch of the New York Public Library on Fifth Avenue at 42nd Street. Considering the size and scope of its collections (49.5 million items, including 17.9 million books) it is amazing that the library is only about one hundred years old. The building, now called the Humanities Library, was designed by Carrère & Hastings and opened with much fanfare in 1911. It is considered the finest example of Beaux-Arts architecture in America. Early in the nineteenth century this lot was the site of a pauper's burying ground and in 1842 an enormous reservoir was built on the spot. The reservoir resembled an Egyptian monument and the fifty-foot-high promenade around the elevated rim became one of the few tourist destinations that far north in Manhattan. In 1899, the reservoir was torn down to make way for the new library building.

Created by the merger of the Astor and Lenox Libraries and the Tilden Trust, with a five million dollar grant for the building from Andrew Carnegie, the library was the fifth largest in the world at the time it was built. Guarding its outside staircase are two large lions carved by Edward C. Potter that have become the symbol for the New York Public Library. Former Mayor La Guardia nicknamed them Patience and Fortitude, and locals always

New York Public Library's lion

New York Public Library, Fifth Avenue, 40th to 42nd Streets

know when Christmas is coming by the large wreaths placed around their necks. In the impressive Astor Hall, the library's lobby, you can schedule a behind-the-scenes tour of the library's inner workings. Visit the wonderful gift shop or the Gottesman Exhibition Hall, a large area displaying constantly changing exhibits. Even if you don't take a tour, make sure to see the newly restored Rose Reading Room on the third floor, one of the largest public rooms in the city. The room's carved ceiling is spectacular.

Also visit the third floor Berg Collection, one of the truly great rare book and manuscript libraries. Among the hundreds of thousands of items are George Washington's handwritten farewell speech to his troops after the Revolution; manuscripts by **Robert Browning** and **T. S. Eliot**, including *The Waste Land;* works by **Thomas Hardy**, **Mark Twain**, and **Virginia Woolf**; a desk belonging to **Charles Dickens**; **Jack Kerouac**'s manuscript scroll of *On the Road,* and much more. Most of the items in this collection were bequeathed by Dr. Albert A. Berg in memory of his brother, Dr. Henry W. Berg, both leading book collectors.

The Algonquin Hotel

49 West 44th Street between Fifth and Sixth Avenues

The Algonquin Hotel and the famous Round Table group of writers are inseparable. Although it opened in 1902, it wasn't until the founding of the Round Table in 1919 that the Algonquin became *the* literary rendezvous in the city, housing writers like **F. Scott Fitzgerald** and journalists **H. L. Mencken, Richard Harding Davis**, and **James Thurber**. That year, a group of newspaper columnists, critics, editors, and playwrights began gathering in the Pergola Room (now the Oak Room) for a weekly luncheon. In 1920, they began to meet daily and were moved to the larger Rose Room, where the luncheons were held for the rest of the decade. Members included **Dorothy Parker, Robert Benchley, Alexander Woollcott, Franklin P. Adams, Harold Ross, Heywood Broun, Robert E. Sherwood, Edna Ferber, George S.**

Alexander Woollcott

Kaufman, Marc Connelly, Donald Ogden Stewart, and **John Peter Toohey**. From time to time other glamorous guests were invited to sit in. **Douglas Fairbanks, Harpo Marx, Tallulah Bankhead, Noel Coward, Alfred Lunt**, and **Lynn Fontanne** all did so at one time or another. The celebrated table can still be found there today.

The group became famous for their sophisticated, chic wit and intelligent conversation punctuated with a sharp-edged sense of humor. Quips and one-liners were their specialties. Robert Benchley, a humorist and actor, who also lived in the hotel, once came in out of the rain and joked, "I'd like to get out of this wet suit and into a dry martini." Dorothy Parker, more famous than the other Round Table members for her sarcasm, once reviewed Katharine Hepburn in an early performance by noting, "She ran the gamut of emotions from A to B." Often their wry humor and stinging wit got them in trouble. When Parker was fired from *Vanity Fair* for writing harsh reviews of some major plays, Benchley and Sherwood resigned in sympathy. Parker and Benchley ended up sharing a small office together of which they said, "had it had one cubic foot less space, it would constitute adultery." Almost everyone knows the famous couplet, "Men seldom make passes / At girls who wear glasses." Not many realize that Parker was its author.

Since many of the members were newspaper columnists, they passed along immediately their antics and barbs to nationwide readers. These

The Algonquin Hotel's Dining Room

writers were the leading columnists at a time when newspaper reader-ship was at its peak and a word from a critic could make or break a book or play. They all wielded tremendous power until the Great Depression brought an end to the Roaring Twenties and the leisure it celebrated, and radio diminished the importance of newspapers. The Round Table members helped shape public opinion in their day much like today's influential television talk show hosts.

Legend has it that *New York Times* drama critic Alexander Woollcott was brought to the hotel by press agent John Peter Toohey to meet Franklin P. Adams and Heywood Broun and to sample the angel food cake. He enjoyed the cake and the conversation so much that he began to take his lunch there on a regular basis. Woollcott, Adams, and Broun were joined by *Vanity Fair* writers Robert E. Sherwood, Dorothy Parker, and Robert Benchley, who began eating together, they said, so that midgets at the Hippodrome theater wouldn't pick on the very tall Sherwood as he walked past. Adams wrote the widely read column "The Conning Tower" for the *New York Tribune;* Broun wrote a column "It Seems to Me" for the *New York World*; George S. Kaufman was a playwright who wrote several of the Marx Brothers comedies, as well as *Dinner at Eight* and *Of Thee I Sing* (the first musical to win the Pulitzer Prize); Harold Ross, along with *New York Times* reporter Jane Grant, launched the *New Yorker* in 1925. The *New Yorker*, dedicated to intelligent, sophisticated writing was a direct outgrowth of the Round Table with many early contributions from these same writers.

Gertrude Stein

After the passing of the Round Table's golden era, the Algonquin still attracted a literary set. **Gertrude Stein** and **Alice B. Toklas** stayed at the hotel when they returned to America in 1934 after twenty-five years abroad. Stein walked from the hotel to Times Square on

William Faulkner

Noël Coward

her first night in the city to see the news of her arrival scrolled in lights above Broadway. **William Faulkner** wrote his 1949 Nobel Prize acceptance speech here on Algonquin stationery. **Gore Vidal, John Updike, Thornton Wilder, Tennessee Williams, Art Buchwald, Bruce Catton, Graham Greene,** and **Brendan Behan** all have stayed here. Behan was the only one asked to leave after he chased the maids through the corridors. **Alan Jay Lerner** and **Frederick Loewe** wrote the musical, *My Fair Lady*, in Room 908.

Having undergone a million-dollar renovation to restore its lobby, the Algonquin once again has a very sophisticated ambience, and it is well worth a visit. Relax and enjoy the atmosphere of days gone by when urbane repartee resounded through the dark wood-paneled rooms. You may even see the hotel cat, Hamlet, the fifth to carry on the name.

Gotham Book Mart

41 West 47th Street

Gotham Book Mart is a true literary landmark. Founded in 1920 at 128 West 45th Street by the erudite and astute **Frances Steloff**, Gotham Book Mart soon became an active center for the literary avant-garde in New York City. The bookstore moved to 51 West 47th Street in 1923 and again, in 1946, to its present home at 41 West 47th Street. When the bookstore was forced from its former location, Steloff thought she might have to close the store permanently, but authors Christopher Morley (who lived across the street) and Mark Van Doren engineered a plan to have her buy the building from Columbia University. As a result, the store has remained in the neighborhood for more than fifty years. From the very beginning the shop emphasized modern literature and poetry and is today one of the few remaining privately owned bookstores in Manhattan. It is identified by a cast-iron sign outside that states: "Wise Men Fish Here." Today, of course, Wise Women are welcome to fish, too.

Photographs of many of the store's notable clientele are displayed around the edges of the rooms. They show favorites such as **W. H. Auden, Elizabeth Bishop, Paul Goodman, Randall Jarrell, Robert Lowell, Marianne Moore, Delmore Schwartz, Dame Edith** and **Sir Osbert Sitwell, Stephen Spender, Gore Vidal, Jose Garcia Villa,** and **Tennessee Williams**.

Gotham Book Mart

Upstairs is a large gallery used for book publication parties and receptions that has hosted everyone from **Allen Ginsberg** to **Anaïs Nin**, **Dylan Thomas**, and **William Carlos Williams**. It was at the Gotham that a "wake," complete with clay pipes and Irish whiskey, was held in 1939 to honor the publication of James Joyce's masterpiece *Finnegan's Wake*. The James Joyce Society was founded in the bookstore in 1947 with T. S. Eliot as the first member.

The legendary bookstore was also a "home away from home" for many writers. They received their mail at the shop, and there was a bulletin board to post notices, on which **Henry Miller** made fre-

Frances Steloff at the Gotham Book Mart

quent appeals for rent money. Steloff was very generous and frequently loaned money to people like Martha Graham and Edmund Wilson. John Dos Passos once left his manuscript for *Manhattan Transfer* as collateral on a two hundred dollar loan. Writers also worked in the store from time to time. Allen Ginsberg lasted only a few days, and LeRoi Jones not much longer—it was too tempting to read than to actually work when surrounded by all those books. The tradition of the great bookstore is continued today by Andreas Brown, who has owned the shop for the past quarter century. Check out the enormous stock of Edward Gorey books or the poetry alcove. Although Gertrude Stein and Ezra Pound are no longer customers, keep your eyes open for the likes of John Updike and Arthur Miller, who are.

Truman Capote's Last Home

870 United Nations Plaza between East 48th and 49th Streets

Truman Capote (1924–1984) lived in an apartment at 870 United Nations Plaza once he had achieved fame and fortune. The building is one of two modern monoliths north of the United Nations built in 1966 to house the IBM World Trade Center. Due to a change in the real estate market, the business offices were changed into apartments before completion and only the lower floors were used for commercial purposes. The address attracted its share of society leaders who came for the excellent views, if not the architecture. Capote was a southern country boy who came to New York City to make his name, and when he did, he

en honor of MRS. Katharine Graham

MR. TRUMAN CAPOTE

REQUESTS THE PLEASURE OF YOUR COMPANY

AT A BLACK AND WHITE DANCE

ON MONDAY, THE TWENTY-EIGHTH OF NOVEMBER

AT TEN O'CLOCK

GRAND BALLROOM, THE PLAZA

R.S.V.P.
MISS ELIZABETH DAVIS
465 ~~485~~ PARK AVENUE
NEW YORK

DRESS
GENTLEMEN: BLACK TIE BLACK MASK
LADIES: BLACK OR WHITE DRESS
WHITE MASK: FAN

Invitation to Truman Capote's Black and White Ball, 1966

chose to live in style. When he moved to this apartment later in his life, he had become identified with the sophisticated high society of New York and enjoyed the snobbery that went with it. His fabulous five-room co-op apartment had floor to ceiling window views. Gloria Steinem described it as "a dusty-plush 'best' parlor in the South seen through the eyes of Vuillard, and suspended twenty stories above Manhattan."

Capote was seventeen when he arrived in New York and lived in various modest apartments around Manhattan and Brooklyn. He found a job as copyboy for the *New Yorker* magazine but was fired for walking out of a reading by poet Robert Frost, who complained to Capote's boss. By 1948, Capote had published his first novel, *Other Voices, Other Rooms*, and was on his way. He made friends easily and mixed with high society in his own flamboyant style, outraging many he met. In 1958, his best-selling *Breakfast at Tiffany's* described a heroine, Holly Golightly, with whom many New Yorkers identified, and fortune followed when the book was made into a popular motion picture. He was established as one of the leading writers of his generation with the 1965 publication of his account of a terrible killing spree, *In Cold Blood*. Capote loved the trappings of fame as much as the writing, and in November 1966 he hosted a masked ball at the Plaza Hotel in honor of Katherine Graham, the publisher of the *Washington Post*. The "Black and White Ball" turned out to be legendary and cost Capote more than $16,000, a princely sum at the time. Everyone from Frank Sinatra and Mia Farrow to Thornton Wilder and Lauren Bacall was there. The party heralded the pattern of Capote's later years, when he appeared on countless television talk shows as a personality and entertaining storyteller rather than a writer. He wrote infrequently. He died while traveling in Los Angeles in 1984.

Turtle Bay Gardens

48th and 49th Streets between Second and Third Avenues

Turtle Bay Gardens is a marvelous enclosed communal garden behind twenty houses that face East 48th and 49th Streets between Second and Third Avenues. The shared gardens form a relaxing retreat from Midtown's hectic pace, and the buildings have attracted their share of celebrities. For no reason other than coincidence, the houses on the East 49th Street side of the gardens have attracted theatrical people, and the houses on the East 48th Street side have attracted the writers.

Most notable of the writers was essayist, fiction writer, and literary stylist, **E. B. White** (1899–1985) and his wife, **Katharine Sergeant**. Katharine was the managing editor for the *New Yorker*, where she met White. They lived at two different addresses during the 1940s and 1950s, first at 239 East 48th Street then at 229 East 48th from 1945 to 1957. From 1936 to 1938, White had lived at 245 East 48th, just outside the garden complex. He wrote dozens of books for adults, among them a collection about this very block, *The Second Tree from the Corner*, and the *New Yorker* influential "Talk of the Town" and "Notes and Comment" columns. But he is best known for two children's books he wrote while living at 229 East 48th Street, *Charlotte's Web* and *Stuart Little*. He was inspired by his summer retreats to Deer Isle in Maine, where he visited the annual Blue Hill Fair, home of Charlotte (a spider).

Columnist **Dorothy Thompson** (1893–1961) also lived in Turtle Bay Gardens, at 237 East 48th Street, after her 1941 divorce from Sinclair Lewis. She wrote an important column for the *New York Herald Tribune* called "On the Record." The apartment was decorated in a Bauhaus style, with a large library and an office filled with maps and a shortwave radio with which she followed the events of World War II. Her columns supported the war effort, but after the war, she fell into disfavor for not being tough enough in her stand against the defeated Germany. She lived here until 1957, the same year that E. B. White moved away. Knopf editor, **Robert Gottlieb**, lived in the same house at one time.

Scribner editor Maxwell Perkins lived at 246 East 49th Street from 1932 to 1938, the years of some of his greatest achievements. He was instrumental in editing the works of Thomas Wolfe for publication as well as the writings of F. Scott Fitzgerald, Ernest Hemingway, Ring Lardner, and Marjorie Kinnan Rawlings.

Theater and music people living on the East 49th Street side of Turtle Bay Gardens included long-time resident Katharine Hepburn, Maggie Smith, Stephen Sondheim, Leopold Stokowski, Ruth Gordon, and Garson Kanin.

E. B. White

Pulitzer Fountain

Grand Army Plaza, Fifth Avenue at 59th Street

The Pulitzer Fountain is actually called the Fountain of Abundance, with the figure of Pomona on top. It was created by the sculptor Karl Bitter and the architectural firm of Carrère and Hastings, and in 1916 was given to the city by Joseph Pulitzer. Located in front of the Plaza Hotel and along Fifth Avenue, New York's most fashionable street, it is a wonderful locale to remember **F. Scott Fitzgerald** (1896–1940) and his wife, Zelda. Scott, as he was known to friends, more than any other writer of the twentieth century, came to be identified with the elegance and sophistication of the city. Alfred Kazin wrote, "Fitzgerald remains the only poet of New York's upper-class landmarks." His novels, such as *The Beautiful and the Damned, The Great Gatsby*, and *Tender Is the Night*, brought fame and fortune but never lasting happiness to Fitzgerald.

In 1919, Fitzgerald arrived in New York City from Minnesota, by way of Princeton. He took a job at an ad agency in order to have enough money to live on while awaiting the publication of his first book, *This Side of Paradise*. Eight days after the book was published, Fitzgerald married his Alabama sweetheart, **Zelda Sayre**, in the rectory of St. Patrick's. The book was an overwhelming critical and popular success, and Scott and Zelda moved into the plush Biltmore Hotel on East 43rd Street. The handsome couple became the toast of the town, loving the night life and living with reckless abandon. They became famous for their drunken parties and excessive lifestyle, as Fitzgerald wrote, "America was going on the greatest, gaudiest spree in history and there was going to be plenty to tell about it." Their lives revolved around

Pulitzer Fountain

parties at the Algonquin, the Knickerbocker, the Ritz, and the Plaza,
with the people that represented the disillusioned "Lost Generation"
that he described in vivid detail. On more than one occasion, fueled by
alcohol, their escapades would end in a midnight dip in the Pulitzer
Fountain. Even though this was during Prohibition, there was no short-
age of alcohol, and especially popular were tea dances at the Plaza and
other hotels, where tea was seldom seen. When the Fitzgeralds could
afford it, they lived at the Plaza, and when they couldn't, they rented an
apartment in a building at 38 West 59th Street and had the Plaza room
service deliver their meals to them. Zelda, a vivacious beauty, was the
original flapper, a model for the new American woman. She set fashion
trends for a decade, but the hectic lifestyle was too much for her, and
by 1930 she was hospitalized with incurable schizophrenia. Fitzgerald
died at the age of forty-four, completely dissipated by alcoholism, his
wife's illness, and the very excesses that he extolled.

The Plaza Hotel

768 Fifth Avenue at 59th Street

In 1955, a precocious literary character was created at the Plaza Hotel, and neither the Plaza nor the world has been the same since. *Eloise* made such an impact on American culture of the 1950s, that the waves she created are still being felt. She was a six-year-old who came to symbolize a new feisty woman for a country that was tired of the restrictions placed on women. She was the Holden Caulfield of countless little girls; her exotic life became their dream. The playwright Wendy Wasserstein credits Eloise with being "my way out of Brooklyn into Manhattan." Eloise gave form to an urbane, sophisticated outlook that represented an imaginary life that the Plaza had to offer, and also heralded the women's rights movement of the 1960s. Eloise was a new kind of heroine for girls brought up on *Rebecca of Sunnybrook Farm* and *The Secret Garden*. She was positively her own woman and she came to define New York in the same way that *Madeline* defined Paris. She created her own world.

The Plaza Hotel

Eloise lived on the top floor of the Plaza, with her nanny, her maid Johanna, her dog named Weenie, and her turtle named Skipperdee. We never see her mother and her father is never mentioned. The staff of the enormous hotel watched over her, and she takes a good deal of watching, for she is full of imagination, pranks, and curiosity. Eloise was created by **Kay Thompson** and illustrated by **Hilary Knight**. Thompson was an actress, singer, and music coach for people like Lena Horne and Judy Garland. During the early 1950s, Thompson sang in the Persian Room at the Plaza and lived in the hotel rent-free. Most people believe that Thompson's inspiration for Eloise came from her close association with Judy Garland's daughter, Liza Minelli, Thompson's goddaughter. But Thompson says that Eloise more closely represents herself. Hilary Knight, a young illustrator, met Thompson through a mutual friend in 1954. Knight sent Thompson a Christmas card with a drawing of a little girl in Santa's pack; that drawing was the birth of Eloise. One of the few children's books to ever make the best-seller lists, it has sold millions of copies and been the inspiration for plays, movies, fashions, and television programs.

Hilary Knight gave the original painting of Eloise to Kay Thompson in 1956 and she, in turn, gave it to the Plaza. The Plaza placed the portrait in the lobby of the hotel, possibly the only fictional character to be honored thus in any public building. The portrait was stolen a few years later, but Mr. Knight replaced it in 1964 at the urging of Jacqueline Kennedy, who brought her two children to the hotel to see the painting. In 1997, the Museum of the City of New York installed a corner of Eloise's room as part of its permanent exhibit. The American Library Association's Friends of Libraries group has placed a brass plaque at the Plaza's door, noting that this is "The Home of Eloise." For readers stuck in the suburbs, Eloise still represents a liberation from the humdrum and commonplace.

Antoine de Saint-Exupéry's Apartment

240 Central Park South at Columbus Circle

$\mathbf{F}$ew people know that among the hundreds of thousands of books written in New York City is one of the most famous French books of all time. *The Little Prince*, by **Antoine de Saint-Exupéry**, was written in an apartment in fashionable 240 Central Park South, while the author was in exile during World War II.

This widely read classic, which has sold over 50 million copies worldwide and still sells 135,000 copies per year in America alone, is loved by children and adults alike. In the story, the aviator is repairing his airplane after crashing in the desert when he meets a little prince. As the aviator draws a picture of a sheep for him, the little prince tells of his journey from planet to planet, of the characters that he meets along the way, and of his relationship with a beautiful rose. It is a fable that can be read on many levels and is more delightful with each reading.

Saint-Exupéry was born in France in 1900 to an

Saint-Exupéry's Apartment

110

aristocratic family. He was well educated and became a pioneer of French aviation, and his courage and heroic exploits became subjects for a series of international best-sellers during the 1930s. These books made him one of the most famous French writers of his time. He flew missions for France over North Africa at the beginning of World War II but with Paris's surrender to German occupation, he chose to exile himself in New York. Saint-Exupéry desperately tried to get back into the fight to free France, but he was forced to remain in New York from 1941 until 1943. He was finally assigned to a French air squadron, even though he was ten years too old and in poor health. On July 31, 1944, he was sent out alone on a reconnaissance flight over Nazi-occupied France and never returned.

During his stay in New York City, he lived in a twenty-third floor apartment overlooking Central Park, drawing and writing *The Little Prince*. Fueled by coffee, cigarettes, and Coca-Cola, he would frequently write all night, both here and at his rented summer home on Long Island. His friends remember him in this

Saint-Exupéry

apartment experimenting with a recipe for a thick green soup made in the bathtub, releasing squadrons of paper airplanes from his balcony over Central Park, tossing water bombs onto the sidewalk below, and blowing enormous glycerin bubbles with a rolled up newspaper. He had a love of life, flying, and France, and most friends felt that his death was exactly as he would have wanted it.

Ernest Hemingway's Hotels

Locations: Hotel Brevoort (Fifth Avenue at Eighth Street, now demolished); Barclay (111 East 48th Street, now Hotel Inter-Continental); Sherry-Netherland (781 Fifth Avenue)

The relationship **Ernest Hemingway** (1899–1961) had with New York City can best be summed up in his own words, "It's a town you come to for a short time." For Hemingway, the city represented not so much a love-hate relationship, as it did for other writers, but a necessary evil. Because New York was the heart of the publishing industry, he had to come to the city to draw up contracts, revise proofs, meet with editors and do publicity, everything he abhorred about the business of writing. It wasn't so much that he hated to do interviews but he wanted to do them on his own terms, and that usually meant taking the reporter on safari, or fishing, or to the top of a mountain. But even in New York, where he was out of his element, he usually demanded to be the center of attention. Hemingway established the pattern he would follow for the rest of his life when he began visiting New York in the early 1920s. He always stayed at the most luxurious hotels, beginning with the Brevoort Hotel on Fifth Avenue at 8th Street. While there he met with **Maxwell Perkins,** his editor at Scribner's, to take care of business. Then he would visit friends, such as fellow Lost Generation writers **F. Scott Fitzgerald** and **Sherwood Anderson.** Often Hemingway would work on galleys and proofs of his books,

The Sherry-Netherland, Fifth Avenue and 59th Street

reading chapters aloud to his friends, revising continually as needed.

In 1940, Hemingway brought the manuscript for his book, *For Whom the Bell Tolls*, to Perkins, then spent ninety-six hours at the Barclay (now the Hotel Inter-Continental) sending corrections to Scribner's via messenger as fast as he could write them. He lived on tea and gin, saw no one until the job was done, and then left the city as quickly as he could.

Ernest Hemingway

In the late 1940s, Hemingway began staying at the Sherry-Netherland, another luxury hotel at 781 Fifth Avenue. That became his favorite hotel because they were able to provide him with the privacy he needed. Hemingway agreed to have a columnist from the *New Yorker*, Lillian Ross, follow him around for a few days in order to write a human interest profile about him in New York. He did his best to impress Ross. He wore orange pajamas, he ordered room service to bring caviar and bottles of Perrier-Jouët Brut, he entertained Marlene Dietrich, whom he called "The Kraut," and he wouldn't leave for appointments until they had emptied all the bottles. On that occasion he was in town to finish work on one of his last major books, *Across the River and Into the Trees*. It was not well-received by the reviewers. In the article, Ross painted an accurate picture of Hemingway's moodiness, similar to the swings in mood that would bring him to suicide a dozen years later. In 1959, Hemingway bought a three-room apartment at 1 East 62nd Street as a retreat for his wife, but he always preferred the protection and anonymity that these prestige hotels could provide. Hemingway died in 1961 of a self-inflicted gunshot wound.

Grolier Club

47 East 60th Street between Park and Madison Avenues

The Grolier Club, at 47 East 60th Street, was named after **Jean Grolier, Vicomte D'Aiguisy** (1479–1565), one of the world's first great bibliophiles. While serving as the French ambassador in Venice during the Renaissance, Grolier became the patron of the printer Aldus, and his large collection contained nearly every book published by the Aldine Press. The goals of the modern Grolier Club, founded in 1884, are no different than Jean Grolier's. They are to foster "the literary study and promotion of the arts pertaining to the production of books." Members love books for their inherent beauty as objects, just as much as they do for their content. Located in a fashionable Upper East Side neo-Georgian townhouse, built in 1917 by architect and club member, Bertram Grosvenor Goodhue, this private club has that comfortable feel of another era with its overstuffed leather chairs and peaceful tranquility. There are exhibitions of the collections (whether illuminated manuscripts, books about Christmas, or collections of works by bookmen such as William Morris and Lewis Carroll) belonging to their members that are open to the public and always interesting.

The club has grown from its original nine members to about 675 men and women. It also holds lectures and conferences on various book-related topics and publishes books on subjects ranging from *Bookbindings, Old and New* to *One Hundred Books Famous in Medicine*. In addition to all this, the Grolier Club has an excellent library of more than 100,000 volumes about printing and other book arts.

The Grolier Club ensignia

Central Park Mall

Central Park near East 67th Street

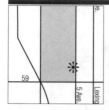

In the late nineteenth century, space was allocated for several literary statues at the south end of the Central Park Mall. The first sculpture to be place here was in 1872, when John Quincy Adams Ward's statue of **William Shakespeare** was unveiled. It was an appropriate choice because Shakespeare is widely considered the greatest writer of the English language. The cornerstone for the statue was actually laid in 1864 to celebrate the 300th anniversary of Shakespeare's birth in 1564. Edwin Booth, America's greatest Shakespearean actor of the time and brother of Lincoln's assassin, John Wilkes Booth, spearheaded the drive to erect the statue, but work was delayed by the Civil War and its aftermath.

A few months later, a group of Scottish Americans erected the statue of **Sir Walter Scott** by Sir John Steell. The statue honored the author of *Ivanhoe* and *The Lady of the Lake* who lived from 1771 to 1832. Scott, who is generally credited as being one of the world's most important historical novelists, is depicted seated on a rock, writing with his faithful dog at his side.

Close by is a sculpture of another great Scottish author, **Robert Burns**. This one was also created by Sir John Steell around 1880. Certainly Scotland's greatest poet, Burns is best known by the general public for his song "Auld Lang Syne (The good old days long past)" sung each New Year's Eve.

The fourth literary figure honored on the Mall is **Fitz-Greene Halleck**. Hardly anyone is familiar with his name today, but such was not the case in 1877 when ten thousand people turned out at the statue's unveiling. Such is the trick of time and fame. President Rutherford B. Hayes and William Cullen Bryant were among the many speakers saluting Halleck on that day. Halleck and **Joseph Rodman Drake** were the creators of "The Croakers," a series of articles which lampooned prominent New York figures in 1819. "The Croakers" became an immediate smash success and so great was the influence of these and subsequent writings that upon Halleck's death a private subscription was founded to collect money for a statue in the writer's honor. There is a monument to his partner Drake in Drake Park in the East Bronx, but today their works are out of print and virtually unknown.

The Mall: Central Park

Alice in Wonderland and Hans Christian Andersen Statues

Central Park near East 75th Street

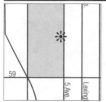

Without a doubt, the most beloved children's literary landmarks in New York City are these two statues on the edge of the Conservatory Pond in Central Park, near Fifth Avenue and 75th Street. Everyone loves to climb on the statues and delights in petting the Dormouse or sitting on Alice's lap. **Lewis Carroll**'s heroine, Alice, was sculpted in 1959 by José de Creeft. George Delacorte donated the sculpture to the city as a memorial to his wife, Margarita, whose favorite quotes from the story encircle the base of the statue. De Creeft used the famous John Tenniel illustrations of Alice and her friends as his model.

Not far away, on the west side of the pond, is the statue of the great Danish storyteller, **Hans Christian Andersen**. Georg John Lober created the statue in 1956 in honor of the 150th anniversary of Andersen's birth. Although his bronze statue is larger than life, it is the small duckling at his feet that attracts the most attention. This is the "Ugly Duckling," of the story known by almost every child. In 1973, young New Yorkers were saddened by the theft of the sixty-pound duckling, but it was recovered from a vacant lot in Queens and securely fastened back in its rightful spot in the park. During the summer, storytelling is provided here on Saturday mornings.

While in this section of the park, you may also want to visit the statue of Mother Goose at the entrance to the Mary Harriman Rumsey Playground near East Drive and 72nd Street. This 1938 statue by George Richard Roth shows Mother Goose riding on her goose, her cloak flying in the wind. It is one of several WPA-sponsored sculptures in the city.

Hans Christian Andersen statue

Delacorte Theater

Central Park near West 81st Street

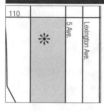

Ⓞne of the favorite summer pastimes for New Yorkers is a picnic in Central Park, followed by an evening of **Shakespeare** under the stars. Producer and director **Joseph Papp** organized the New York Shakespeare Festival in 1954 in a church in the East Village and began giving free performances in Central Park on a temporary stage in 1957. In 1959, a well-publicized battle to force the festival out of the park took place between New York parks commissioner Robert Moses and Joseph Papp. Moses lost the fight and although Papp died in 1991, his legacy continues.

In 1962, publisher **George Delacorte,** Jr., built the Delacorte Theater at the edge of the Great Lawn as a permanent stage for the festival. Delacorte, the founder of Dell paperback books, sold the firm to Doubleday in 1976, and turned his attention and resources to philanthropic works. Since the early 1960s, two plays have been produced each summer, usually classics by Shakespeare, although other plays like Gilbert and Sullivan operettas or *On the Town* are occasionally staged. Many well-known actors and actresses have played the roles to enthusiastic audiences.

William Shakespeare

Delacorte Theater

Some of these productions have gone on to Broadway and Off Broadway theaters, such as *The Pirates of Penzance* with Kevin Kline and *The Tempest* with Patrick Stewart.

Tickets are distributed in a fair and organized manner. On the day of the performance, free tickets are distributed at the both the Delacorte Theater and the Public Theater on Lafayette Street. The Delacorte Theater is open-air, similar in that way to the theaters of Shakespeare's day. Spend some time looking around outside the theater before the performance begins and you'll find two wonderful sculptures based on Shakespeare's plays *The Tempest* and *Romeo and Juliet*. These were also donated to the city by Delacorte and are works of artist Milton Hebald who created *The Tempest* in 1966 and *Romeo and Juliet* in 1977. On the hill behind the theater is a Shakespearean garden that contains almost every variety of plant mentioned in his work.

John Steinbeck's House

175 East 78th Street between Lexington and Third Avenues

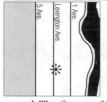

Born in Salinas, California, **John Steinbeck** (1902–1968), is the Monterey Peninsula's favorite son. His works, such as *Cannery Row, East of Eden,* and *The Grapes of Wrath* are so rich with California that many people forget that he spent almost half of his life in New York City. His association with the city began in 1925, when he moved in with his sister. For a few weeks he earned money by pushing wheelbarrows of cement during the construction of the old Madison Square Garden. It was at that time he began to write stories, though he had no luck finding a publisher for them. He returned to California the following year and while there he had much more success publishing works such as *Of Mice and Men* and *Tortilla Flat*. In 1941, after winning the Pulitzer Prize for *The Grapes of Wrath*, he moved again to Manhattan where he lived at several addresses until his death in December 1968.

Early in 1946, while his wife Gwyn was pregnant with their second son, the Steinbecks purchased the two houses at 175–177 East 78th Street and began making renovations. They intended to live in 175 and rent out 177 to friends and share the common garden in back. They rented to Nathaniel and Marjorie Benchley. Nathaniel was Robert Benchley's son and a well-known author himself. Like Gwyn, Marjorie was also pregnant and had one boy already, Peter, who would grow up to write *Jaws*. The Steinbecks and the Benchleys had much in common as their families expanded. While the renovations on the house continued, John Steinbeck moved in to his office in the basement to work on his, *The Wayward Bus*. He wrote to a friend that "the working cellar is fine— gray concrete walls and cement floor and pipes overhead. A comfortable chair and desk and filing cabinet in which I hope to file bills so I can find them. All fine—no window, no ability to look out and watch the postman and garbage wagon."

In the spring of 1947, Steinbeck had a piano moved into the house. It was lifted from the street to the second-story window, from which a hip-high railing had been removed. The railing was not replaced very well and when Steinbeck leaned on it, it gave way. He fell, seriously injuring his knee and foot. After spending weeks in the hospital he had to use a cane for the better part of the next year. This was not his only misfortune during his stay here. In August 1948, his wife asked for a divorce. He was forced to sell the house in 1949, and he moved to another house at 206 East 72nd Street, which is no longer standing. There, he wrote his great novel *East of Eden*; bought a large black poodle named Charley, who became the subject of his last book, *Travels with Charley*, and received the Nobel Prize for Literature.

Steinbeck was always of two minds about New York. He never really got over his negative feelings about the city that had rejected him in the 1920s. In "The Making of a New Yorker" he wrote that New York was "an ugly city, a dirty city" but he did concede that "once you have lived in New York . . . no place else is good enough." While living on East 78th Street, he wrote to a good friend, "New York is a wonderful city. I'm glad to be putting down some kind of roots here. It is going to be the capital of the world. It isn't like the rest of the country—it's like a nation itself—more tolerant than the rest in a curious way . . . neither good nor bad but unique."

John Steinbeck

123

Bemelmans Bar at the Hotel Carlyle

35 East 76th Street at Madison Avenue

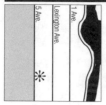

Although **Ludwig Bemelmans** was born and spent his childhood in the Tyrol and southern Germany, he emigrated to New York City in 1914 at the age of seventeen and lived most of his life here. When he arrived, he began working in elegant hotels, beginning as a busboy and working his way up to an assistant manager at the Ritz-Carlton. He also sketched his fellow employees and clientele alike, frequently on the backs of hotel menus, molding them into characters that would later fill the pages of newspaper and magazine articles and his own books. He is most famous for his award-winning series of children's books featuring *Madeline,* the little copper-haired scamp who was one of twelve orphan

Bemelmans Bar at the Carlyle

girls living in a convent. "In an old house in Paris / that was covered with vines / lived 12 little girls in two straight lines . . . " begins the story of *Madeline*, published in 1939.

Bemelmans became successful as an artist and cartoonist for the *New Yorker* and other magazines of the day, and wrote dozens of fiction and nonfiction books as well. In 1947, he was commissioned to paint murals for the Hotel Carlyle bar, in exchange for which he and his wife Madeleine and daughter Barbara were given a suite of rooms for a

Ludwig Bemelmans

year and a half. He painted murals in many places during his career as an artist, but these are the only ones to survive. They have become so famous that the bar has been named in his honor. They show a world in which humans are kept in zoo cages in Central Park and on Sunday afternoons the animals stroll through the park looking at them. This is just the sort of topsy-turvy world that has made Bemelmans's work so popular for the past sixty years.

The Secret Garden

Central Park, Conservatory Garden at East 105th Street

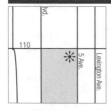

If you venture far enough north on the Fifth Avenue side of Central Park, you will come to the Conservatory Garden at East 105th Street. These formal gardens are often listed as among the most beautiful, relaxing, and inspirational parts of the city. Perhaps it is due to the contrast between the hustle and bustle just outside the gates on the city streets and the calm found inside. This is an elegant, six-acre formal garden with flowering trees and shrubs, fountains, and perennial borders. Here in the gardens, to the left of the gate, is the perfect setting for a statue honoring

Secret Garden statue

Frances Hodgson Burnett's story *The Secret Garden*, placed here when the Conservatory Garden opened in 1936, at the height of the Great Depression.

The Secret Garden tells the story of two young cousins, Mary and Colin, who discover a locked garden in a gloomy old manor on the Yorkshire moors of England. They transform the garden into a paradise and as they do so their own youthful vitality and spirit returns. The sculptor, Bessie Potter Vonnoh, creates a peaceful scene here in this "secret garden" with Colin playing a flute and Mary holding a seashell while listening to the music. At her feet is a gentle fountain, a peaceful setting for a quiet afternoon enjoying the flowers and birds of Central Park. The area was especially designed for reading and storytelling, and hosts its share of weddings as well. The inscription reads "Fountain group given to the children of the city in the name of Frances Hodgson Burnett 1849–1924."

Dante Square

Broadway at West 64th Street

Dante Square sits directly in front of Lincoln Center for the Performing Arts at Broadway and West 64th Street. Long before construction began on Lincoln Center in 1959, this park was created by a group of Italian Americans to honor Italy's greatest poet, **Dante Alighieri** (1265–1321). It was the idea of Carlo Barsotti, the editor of the Italian newspaper *Il Progresso*, to erect a statue honoring Dante in 1912. Originally, the statue was intended to be much more elaborate and was to be placed in Times Square. Earlier Barsotti had helped raise funds for the statues of Italians like Christopher Columbus, Garibaldi, Verdi, and Verrazano, which are found in other city parks. Many people believed that Barsotti's efforts were self-serving, and as a result it wasn't until 1921 that a much more modest statue was unveiled here.

Sculptor Ettore Ximenes worked out a design based on the traditional image of an austere Dante, dressed in robes and crowned with a laurel wreath. In his hand he holds a copy of his most important work, *The Divine Comedy*. This was the first vernacular epic written in the Italian language instead of Latin. It is the story of a trip through heaven and hell, presenting a changeless universe ordered by God, and was written more than six hundred years before the dedication of this statue. Dante's life, like the placement of the statue here, is filled with politics and controversy. He lived much of his life in exile from his native Florence due to his political ideas and was not appreciated by his hometown until long after his death.

Dante statue

Hotel des Artistes

1 West 67th Street between Central Park West and Columbus Avenues

The Hotel des Artistes, at 1 West 67th Street, between Central Park West and Columbus Avenue, is the most famous building on a block originally filled with artists' studios. Over the years, it has been the home of Howard Chandler Christy, who painted the murals in the adjoining Cafe des Artistes, one of the most fashionable restaurants in the city. Christy was the most successful commercial artist of his day, specializing in scantily clothed or nude women, and his spicy illustrations gave birth to the concept of the idealized woman, the "Christy Girl," the model for today's pinup girl. Another long-lived artist, Norman Rockwell, who did not always live in quaint New England towns, in fact was a native New Yorker and had his studio here. The entertainment world was represented as well by the most famous resident of the hotel, Rudolph Valentino, and William Powell and ZaSu Pitts.

Originally the building did not have individual kitchens and the cost of employing a chef was figured into the building's maintenance fee. Meals were delivered to the rooms by a series of dumbwaiters throughout the building, thus eliminating the need for each apartment to have a cook, but the studios were soon renovated to include kitchens.

A sensational event involving the literati took place here was on December 10, 1929. Thirty-one-year-old **Harry Crosby**, bohemian poet and publisher of the Black Sun Press in Paris, who was the nephew of J. P. Morgan, was involved in a double suicide, or murder-suicide. He and his lover Josephine Bigelow were found dead in a friend's ninth-floor studio. Black Sun had been early publishers of **Hart Crane**, **T. S. Eliot**,

James Joyce, and D. H. Lawrence. Crosby's wife, Caresse, was at the theater with Hart Crane at the time of Harry's suicide. The event was immortalized in a poem by e.e. cummings:

> 2 boston
>
> Dolls; found with
>
> Holes in each other
>
> 's lullaby.

Other writers lived here more peacefully. A very successful writer of popular fiction, **Fannie Hurst**, lived here from 1932 until her death in 1968. Also known for her lighthearted style was **Carolyn Wells Houghton**, whose humor books and mysteries like "The Rubaiyat of a Motor Car" were best-sellers of her day.

After Rudolph Valentino, perhaps the most famous resident of the Hotel des Artistes was **Noël Coward.** His plays helped to define the elegant world of New York's high society in which he lived. Alexander Woollcott, the influential theater critic who helped organize the Algonquin Round Table group, and who wrote for the *New Yorker* and hosted the popular radio program "The Town Crier" dur-

Edna Ferber

ing the 1930s, was a resident for a short time. **Edna Ferber** lived and wrote here. Her publisher advised her to move to New York City and rewrite some of her popular stories for the stage. Her novel *Show Boat* was turned into the musical by Jerome Kern and she worked with George S. Kaufman on *Dinner at Eight* and *Stage Door.* Frederick S. Dellenbaugh, who explored the Grand Canyon with Major John W. Powell and wrote an account of the expedition entitled *Breaking the Wilderness*, lived a much less rugged life here. Quite a bit of history is packed into this building.

J. D. Salinger's Boyhood Home

390 Riverside Drive at West 111th Street

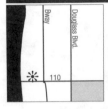

The large apartment building at 390 Riverside Drive on the corner of West 111th Street is the boyhood home of the most elusive of American writers, **J. D. Salinger**, the author of *The Catcher in the Rye*. This book appealed to so many adolescents coming of age in mid-twentieth-century America that the pressures of fame and demands on the author were just too great for him to bear. Salinger moved in 1953 to Cornish, New Hampshire, where he lives in seclusion to this day. He hasn't published a word since 1965.

Salinger appears to have been a boy much like the boys he wrote about in his books. His parents, Sol and Marie Salinger, were an upper-middle-class couple who ran a Kosher cheese importing business and wanted the best for their family, which also included a daughter, Doris, eight years older than "Sonny," as J. D. was nicknamed. In 1919, Jerome David Salinger was born and shortly after the family moved to 390 Riverside Drive. By all accounts, he was a solemn, polite child, who liked to take long walks by himself through the city. He attended public schools where he was an average student in most subjects except arithmetic, which he disliked passionately. He attended the McBurney School, a prestigious private school in the city, for a year before flunking out. From there he was sent to the Valley Forge Military Academy in Pennsylvania at the age of fifteen. Valley Forge was to become the model for Holden Caulfield's school, Pencey Prep in *The Catcher in the Rye*, Salinger's only novel.

The Catcher in the Rye, published in 1951, is the story of a spirited, rebellious, sixteen-year-old boy who runs away from prep school and spends his Christmas break as a free spirit in Manhattan. He loses both his innocence and his virginity in one of the most popular American novels of the twentieth century. Because the action is set mainly in New York City, it is fun to follow Holden's footsteps around town—from Penn Station to Central Park's bandshell and carousel, the American Museum of Natural History, and the skating rink at Rockefeller Center. It is easy to imagine that all these places were remembered by Salinger through his own boyhood walks around the city.

While on Riverside Drive, walk just a block south to number 380—the entrance to the building is around the corner on West 110th Street. This was one of the buildings used by Salinger as the home of his fictional Glass family, whose stories are collected in *Franny and Zooey*, *A Perfect*

Day for Bananafish, *Raise High the Roof Beam, Carpenters*, and *Seymour: An Introduction*. Here the Glass children played curb marbles and stoopball, just as young Salinger no doubt did under the canopy lit by "bulby bright lights."

The Glass family's apartment building

Cathedral of St. John the Divine

1047 Amsterdam Avenue at West 112th Street

The largest church in the United States and the third largest church in the world, after Our Lady at Yamasoukro in the Ivory Coast and St. Peter's in Rome, is the Cathedral of St. John the Divine on Morningside Heights, overlooking Harlem. The cornerstone was laid in 1892, and the church has been under continual construction ever since. The construction process has outlived many of the architects and firms that have taken part in the building over the years. The original design was by the firm of Heins and La Farge, but many alterations have taken place and the process of building by hand in the traditional manner may

Cathedral of Saint John the Divine

go on for another century. Even though it is not complete, the cathedral is very impressive. The main section is over 600 feet long and 124 feet high, with beautiful stained glass windows and marble sculptures everywhere. Over the years, the cathedral has become known for its progressive community outreach programs and literature and the arts have commanded a leading role in the church's activities.

Modeled after the Poet's Corner in Westminster Abbey, St. John's Poet's Corner is devoted to American writers who have achieved a certain degree of fame through their work. The second chapel on the left side was dedicated on November 27, 1983 by St. John's first poet-in-residence, **Daniel Haberman**, and is paved with stones honoring the authors. New names have been added on a regular basis. Today, there are more than thirty writers immortalized. Among the writers' names

Robert Frost

are famous ones such as **Emily Dickinson, F. Scott Fitzgerald, Robert Frost, Langston Hughes, Herman Melville, Henry David Thoreau, Mark Twain, Edith Wharton, Walt Whitman,** and **William Carlos Williams,** plus a few surprises like **Louise Bogan, Anne Bradstreet,** and **Elizabeth Bishop.** Below the name of each author is a line from one of their works. In keeping with these honors, memorial services for writers are frequently held in the great hall of the church. A service was held in the church after **W. H. Auden**'s death in 1973, one of the few poets honored here who was actually a member of the Episcopal Church. Similar services were held after the deaths of Nobel Laureate **Joseph Brodsky** and **Allen Ginsberg**. At Ginsberg's memorial service, more than three thousand mourners listened to tributes and performances by his friends, Philip Glass, Patti Smith, and Natalie Merchant.

Columbia University

Broadway at West 116th Street

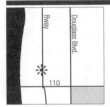

Columbia University, located on Morningside Heights, is one of the oldest, largest, and richest colleges in the country. In 1754, it was founded with only eight students as King's College. It was located downtown near Trinity Church. Early graduates at King's College included patriots like Alexander Hamilton, who was the first Secretary of the Treasury; John Jay who became the first Chief Justice of the United States; Gouverneur Morris, the author of the final draft of the U.S. Constitution; and **Robert R. Livingston**, who administered the oath of office to George Washington. Theodore Roosevelt and Franklin D. Roosevelt were also students here, and Dwight Eisenhower was President of Columbia just before becoming President of the country.

Butler Library is truly one of the greatest libraries in America containing more than seven million volumes and one of the best rare book rooms in New York. Among its treasures are cuneiform tablets, early editions of **Aristotle** and **Euclid**; manuscripts by **Milton, Newton,** and **Washington Irving**; and diaries of George Washington. More contemporary items include **Edgar Allan Poe**'s manuscript for his last poem, "Annabel Lee," Hart Crane's manuscript for

Columbia University

"The Bridge," the original manuscripts of **Tennessee Williams**'s *A Streetcar Named Desire*, **Herman Wouk**'s *The Caine Mutiny,* and even an early typed copy of Allen Ginsberg's "Howl."

Columbia is the only college in the country that can be credited with sparking a literary movement, for it was on this campus that the Beat Generation was born. **Jack Kerouac** and **Allen Ginsberg** were both students at Columbia in the 1940s. They lived in various dorm rooms on campus and several apartments near campus over the years and this is where they met **William Burroughs**, **Neal Cassady**, and **Lucien Carr**. (**Lawrence Ferlinghetti** and **John Clellon Holmes** were also students at Columbia, but they didn't meet the other members of the Beat movement until years later.) Both Kerouac and Ginsberg were inspired by English teachers like Lionel Trilling, Mark Van Doren, and Raymond Weaver.

One student, **Federico Garcia Lorca,** came here for one year only. At the time, he was already one of the most famous poets of Spain and he found everything about New York, from the squalor to the riches, fascinating. He stayed in dorm rooms at John Jay and Furnald Halls during his time here, but his real classroom was the city itself. Although he told his parents that he was doing well learning English, the truth is he learned very little. "Ice cream" and "Times Square" were about the only phrases he ever learned to say. He visited Hart Crane in Brooklyn one night and although they couldn't understand each other's language, they got along well. On the day the stock market crashed in 1929, Lorca went to Wall Street and witnessed for himself the personal disasters resulting from the panic. In 1930, he left school to visit Cuba and never returned to New York, but always considered his nine months in the city to be "the most useful experience of my life." During this time he came to grips with his fame, homosexuality, and writing.

It is difficult to list all the writers who attended Columbia as students or worked as faculty. One of the leading writers of the Harlem Renaissance, Zora Neale Hurston, studied under anthropologist Franz Boas. Bernard Malamud was a student here, as were John Erskine, Herbert Gold, Langston Hughes, Thomas Merton, J. D. Salinger, and Herman Wouk.

Langston Hughes' House

20 East 127th Street

The greatest writer of the Harlem Renaissance was **Langston Hughes** (1902–1967). In 1947, he moved to 20 East 127th Street, where he spent the last twenty years of his life. During this period he wrote books such as *I Wonder as I Wander* and *The Panther and the Lash*. Originally from a poor family, Hughes came to New York in 1921 to attend Columbia University, but for economic reasons he never graduated. Slowly, his work began to be published in magazines like *Opportunity: A Journal of Negro Life* and W. E. B. Du Bois's *Crisis*. In addition to poetry Hughes wrote plays and short stories. In fact, one of his plays, *Mulatto*, ran on Broadway for two years. After years of living in rented rooms and borrowed apartments, he finally had enough income to put a down payment on this brownstone. For years Hughes had been taken care of by an older couple, "Aunt" Toy and "Uncle" Emerson Harper. They were like parents to him, and the house was purchased under their names with money Hughes earned from *Street Scene*. Langston always referred to this house as "Aunt Toy's house." They paid $12,500 for the 1869 row house when they purchased it in 1947 from one of the last members of what had been a small Finnish community. Aunt Toy rented out rooms to boarders in order to meet the expenses, and Langston himself had two rooms and a bath of his own on the third floor overlooking the garden in back. "There is even a beautiful lawn in the back under tall trees . . . cool and restful, sort of like some of the gardens in Greenwich Village," he wrote. He used the house as the setting for several of his stories, including the "third floor rear" apartment of Jesse B. Semple, his most famous character.

Hughes had rejected Aunt Toy's idea of living on fashionable Sugar Hill, where all the wealthy and famous black Harlemites resided. He wanted to be "one of the people" and live in the heart of Harlem on the flats with the common man, instead of with the elite. "I would rather have a kitchenette in Harlem, than a mansion in Westchester," he wrote to a friend. During the 1930s, Hughes became interested in socialism and the cause of the working class, visited Russia, and joined the local John

Langston Hughes' house

Reed Club. These activities led the House Un-American Activities Committee to investigate Hughes, and he was blacklisted from speaking on many college campuses.

While living in this house, Hughes had a simple routine. His day began around noon, when he awoke coughing due to his chain-smoking habit; after a cup of coffee he showered and shaved, then had breakfast prepared by Aunt Toy as his secretary read him the mail. In the afternoons, he worked on correspondence or entertained visitors. Late at night, around 10 or 11 PM, he hit the streets and returned after the bars closed at 2 AM. It was then that he wrote in the peaceful quiet of the night until dawn, when he went out for the morning paper. Afterward, he went to bed, sleeping through the morning hours.

His poetry created a style based on the rhythms of blues, and it was imitated by many other poets. Hughes became one of the few writers of the Harlem Renaissance group to remain prominent after the 1930s. He died from complications while recovering from surgery at age sixty-five .

Schomburg Center for Research in Black Culture

515 Malcolm X Boulevard between West 135th and 136th Streets

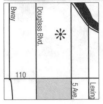

One of the best collections in the world devoted to materials documenting the history and culture of people of African descent is the Schomburg Center for Research in Black Culture, located at 515 Malcolm X Boulevard, between West 135th and West 136th Streets in Harlem. Arthur Schomburg, born in 1874 in San Juan, Puerto Rico, formed the collection. He became interested in the Puerto Rican and Cuban independence movements in the 1890s and from his earliest years he was a bibliophile who collected everything related to African-American culture. This wasn't easy on his meager wages as a messenger for the Bankers Trust Company, but he managed to amass one of the greatest collections of black cultural items at a time when no one else was interested in the subject of the black experience. Schomburg corresponded with **W .E. B. Du Bois**, **John Edward Bruce**, and **James Weldon Johnson** even before he moved to Harlem in 1891. In 1911, Schomburg was elected an officer in the Negro Society for Historical Research and helped form the Negro Book Exchange.

Schomburg Center

In 1926, Schomburg sold his collection to the Carnegie Corporation and became the curator of that collection a few years later, until his death in 1938. He continued to collect and donate material to the library all his life. His materials included books, periodicals, manuscripts, photographs and other documents that tell the history of black and African people around the world. Exhibitions of special interest are always on display, and the research center is open to the public.

The Schomburg Center, a new building to house the Schomburg Collection, opened in 1978. Outside its Langston Hughes Auditorium is a terrazzo floor decorated with the words of Hughes's famous poem, "The Negro Speaks of Rivers." Originally, Schomburg's collection had been housed next door in an art moderne building that was also the 135th Street Branch of the Public Library. All the great names from the Harlem Renaissance gave readings in that building and **Countee Cullen, Claude McKay,** and **Langston Hughes** spent a great deal of time studying there. In 1942, the collection moved to the Countee Cullen Branch of the Public Library at 104 West 136th Street.

W .E. B. Du Bois

American Academy of Arts and Letters

633 West 155th Street at Broadway

The most prestigious honor society for creative artists in this country is the American Academy of Arts and Letters. Its headquarters is in a remote cul-de-sac of important museums and associations known as Audubon Terrace at Broadway and West 155th Street. The land was once part of John James Audubon's estate and his grave is in the cemetery across the street. Archer Milton Huntington donated the Academy building and the architectural firm of McKim, Mead and White designed it in 1923. In 1930, Cass Gilbert designed one of the finest small auditoriums in the city for the Academy. It is used for annual meetings, lectures, and concerts.

In 1898, the National Institute of Arts and Letters was founded by the American Social Science Association to foster, assist, and sustain an interest in literature, music, and the fine arts. In 1904, the American Academy of Arts and Letters was created as an elite body of the institute. In 1976, the two organizations merged under a single board into the National Institute of Arts and Letters and the American Academy of Arts and Letters, but retained two separate memberships. Finally, in 1992, the two groups unified into a single body of 250 members, each elected for life.

American Academy of Arts and Labors

142

William S. Burroughs and Alene Lee, 1953

Members in the department of literature have comprised a who's who of American letters. Early members included **Pearl S. Buck, e.e. cummings, John Dos Passos, William Faulkner, Lillian Hellman, William Dean Howells, Christopher Isherwood, William** and **Henry James, Carl Sandburg, John Steinbeck, Mark Twain, Edith Wharton, Thornton Wilder,** and **Thomas Wolfe.** More recently the Academy has honored writers such as **William S. Burroughs, Truman Capote, Allen Ginsberg, Norman Mailer, Arthur Miller, Toni Morrison, John Updike,** and **Kurt Vonnegut.**

The building houses a gallery, library, and museum which are open to the public for various exhibits. Copies of books and manuscripts by members past and present are available by appointment for research. Every spring the annual meeting of the Academy is attended by most of the current members, and a group portrait of the distinguished gathering is taken, followed by a public reception. Carved into the cornice of the building is the motto: "All arts are one, all branches on one tree . . . Hold high the flaming torch from age to age."

Edgar Allan Poe's Cottage

Grand Concourse on the Southeast corner of East Kingsbridge Road, Bronx

Grand Concourse

Certainly one of the most tragic figures of American literature was **Edgar Allan Poe** (1809–1849), and some of the worst times of his short life took place in a little cottage that still stands in the Fordham section of the Bronx. Poe, originally from Boston, was a short story writer and a poet who occasionally wrote criticism for newspapers and magazines. A true lit-erary genius, he is remembered for the poems "The Raven" and "The Bells" and for a wide range of short sto-ries such as "The Pit and the Pendulum" and "The Fall of the House of Usher." Poe was the mas-ter of the macabre and the mysterious, and his story, "The Murders in the Rue Morgue," is con-sidered the first detective story ever written.

During his lifetime, Edgar Allan Poe was not successful as a writer. He

Edgar Allan Poe

Edgar Allan Poe's cottage

was involved in several costly legal battles and drank heavily. He suffered poor health and financial destitution as a result of all these factors. Poe moved from one cheap boardinghouse or apartment to another, usually just one step ahead of his creditors, and lived in squalor in several different locations in New York City. In the spring of 1846 he moved to a tiny Bronx cottage, which was moved from its original location a block or two away in 1913 to avoid demolition when the road was widened.

Poe moved here with hopes that the more tranquil and clean rural setting would restore the health of his wife Virginia, who was very ill at the time. One visitor wrote about the sad scene: "The weather was cold and the sick lady had the dreadful chills that accompany the hectic fever of consumption. She lay on the straw bed wrapped in her husband's great coat, with a large tortoise-shell cat on her bosom. The wonderful cat seemed conscious of her great usefulness. The coat and the cat were the sufferer's only means of warmth, except as her husband held her hands." Virginia died of tuberculosis in this cottage during the winter of 1847 at age twenty-six. Poe continued to live here with his mother-in-law, Mrs. Maria Clemm, and died while visiting Baltimore in 1849.

Poe wrote many of his most famous works, including "Annabel Lee," "Ulalume," "The Cask of Amontillado," and "The Bells," while living in the cottage. This last was said to have been inspired by the sound of the bell from the University Church at nearby Fordham University. Inside the cottage, memorabilia on display includes the bed in which his wife died and Poe's rocking chair and mirror. Virginia Poe was buried in the neighborhood but in 1878 her remains were taken to Baltimore to rest beside her husband's.

Norman Mailer's Apartment

142 Columbia Heights at Pineapple Street, Brooklyn Heights

Norman Mailer is one of the most colorful contemporary writers in New York City. He has been arrested for the attempted murder of his wife, he has run for mayor, he has been an amateur boxer, and he has written some of the best books of the second half of the twentieth century. Born in 1923, his first novels, *The Naked and the Dead* and *The Deer Park*, quickly established him as one of the leaders in post-World War II literature. His thirst for publicity and his confrontational stance have kept his name in the news for the past fifty years.

There are a dozen buildings in New York that can claim Mailer as a previous resident. In the 1950s he lived in the East Village and Greenwich Village. For the past four decades he has lived in Brooklyn Heights; today he lives at 142 Columbia Heights on the upper floors of this beautiful building on the Brooklyn Heights promenade. He designed a very unusual living and working space meant to resemble the rigging of a ship's forecastle. The only way to move from one part of the loft to another is by means of a

Norman Mailer's Apartment

series of climbing ropes, boarding nets, deck ladders, and catwalks suspended high above the floor.

Mailer has won two Pulitzer Prizes for *The Armies of the Night* in 1968 and for *The Executioner's Song* in 1979. While researching the life of Gary Gilmore, the executed killer that the second book is about, Mailer became friends with Jack Abbott, a jailhouse writer. Mailer helped Abbott win his release from prison in 1981 with the aid of many literary friends, only to have Abbott murder a waiter in an East Village restaurant a few weeks after his release.

While in Brooklyn Heights, take time to walk along the promenade and view the entrancing skyline of Manhattan. Also in Mailer's immediate neighborhood are former homes of W. H. Auden at 1 Montague Street, Thomas Wolfe at 5 Montague Street, Arthur Miller at 155 Willow Street, Truman Capote in the basement of 70 Willow Street, and Hart Crane at 77 Willow Street. No longer standing is 110 Columbia Heights, formerly home to Hart Crane and John Dos Passos. Washington Roebling, who built the Brooklyn Bridge, once lived in the same building. Quite a coincidence, since Hart Crane's most famous poem was "The Bridge."

Richard Wright's House

175 Carlton Avenue between Myrtle and Willoughby Avenues,
Fort Greene, Brooklyn

Richard **Wright** (1908–1960), was born in Mississippi, died in Paris, told stories focusing on Chicago
and the South, but nevertheless wrote his greatest
work, *Native Son*, in a renovated house that still
stands at 175 Carlton Avenue in Brooklyn. He had been living in New
York for several years working for the Federal Writers Project of
the WPA when, in 1939, he received a Guggenheim Fellowship that
enabled him to take time away from his job to write *Native Son*. It soon
became one of the most popular books by a black author in America, a
popularity which has increased over the years. Wright continued to live
in various New York apartments for several more years, but he left

America after World War II for
Paris, where he spent the rest of
his life. Without a doubt, Wright
was the most prominent African-
American writer of his generation, and countless younger writers, from Gwendolyn Brooks to
James Baldwin, asked for his
advice and support. In his later
years, Wright was harassed by
the FBI and CIA due to his
membership in the Communist
Party during the 1930s and early
1940s, the period when he lived
on Carlton Avenue.

Richard Wright

148

Wright lived in the house in the Fort Greene section of Brooklyn with his wife and child. His routine for working was to get up as early as 5:30 AM, and during the summer climb to the top of the hill in nearby Fort Greene Park to write. Around 10 AM he would return to his house for breakfast, after which he would type up what he had written in the park. His friends, Jane and Herbert Newton, also lived in the same house, and when they moved, he moved first to a house which is no longer standing at 522 Gates Avenue, then to a brownstone still there at 87 Lefferts Place. By that time, *Native Son* was finished, and Wright and his friends took turns reading the book aloud to the background music of Shostakovich played as loud as possible. In 1943, he moved to an apartment next door at 89 Lefferts Place where he stayed for two years. *Native Son* was so popular that Orson Welles and John Houseman asked Wright to adapt it for the stage, and in 1941 the play opened on Broadway at the St. James Theater. In 1947, when negotiations for a movie contract were underway, Hollywood moguls insisted that the main character, Bigger Thomas, be depicted as a white man. Wright refused, knowing that the whole point of the story would be lost. Instead Wright made a low-budget film in which he played the role of Bigger himself. It took another forty years before Hollywood had the courage to tackle the theme.

Arthur Miller's Boyhood Homes

1277 Ocean Parkway between Avenues L and M and 1350 East 3rd Street just off Avenue M, Sheepshead Bay, Brooklyn

One of our greatest contemporary playwrights, **Arthur Miller**, was born on West 111th Street in Manhattan in 1915. While in his teens, he and his family moved from the Upper West Side out to a neighborhood in far-off Brooklyn. The move was to make a lasting impression on Miller and affect his writing and personal philosophy. The Millers' first home in Brooklyn was a modest house that still stands at 1277 Ocean Parkway. They lived here briefly and moved across Ocean Parkway to a nearby dead-end street at 1350 East 3rd Street, just north of Avenue M. The one- and two-family dwellings, originally made of wood, were cheaply built after World War I and those who wanted to escape the congestion of the city could afford to live here at the time. The Millers considered this house the home of their dreams. Miller loved the neighborhood and said of it, "one belongs somewhere, a well-oriented, well-grounded sense of touch, a sense of history, people growing older, people getting married, careers. It was a stable, ongoing, articulated community in a sense that the suburb today is not. I'm glad I grew up that way. It never leaves you."

This house became the setting for Miller's greatest play, *Death of a Salesman*. It was here that Willy Loman, a

Arthur Miller

traveling salesman, returned from his lonely trips on the road deluded into believing that he was well-liked by everyone. On stage, Loman's career ended turbulently in this house and he realized that his perfect world was make-believe. Fortunately, the Millers lived a happier life here than did Willy Loman. Arthur Miller remembers that his mother didn't venture into Manhattan more than once or twice a year because she felt safe and secure in their small community and didn't miss the fast pace of the city. They had a tomato garden in the backyard, and Miller and his friends roamed the surrounding fields looking for snakes and rabbits. The area continued to be developed, and most of its small-town atmosphere is now gone, but you can still feel it on this street, away from the traffic of Ocean Parkway. Miller wrote an autobiography, *Timebends* in 1988; it documents his life in Brooklyn.

Miller left Brooklyn to attend the University of Michigan, where he decided to become a writer. He returned to Brooklyn and lived for many years at a dozen different addresses, mostly around Brooklyn Heights, where in 1947 he wrote his first play to reach Broadway, *All My Sons*. Two years later he wrote *Death of a Salesman* while living at 31 Grace Court in Brooklyn Heights, winning both a Pulitzer Prize and a Tony Award. After that success, the critics cooled to his plays and were openly hostile to his 1964 play, *After the Fall*, which was based on his marriage to Marilyn Monroe. In recent years, revivals of his plays have met with enthusiastic reviews, and he is again considered a giant of the American theater.

Index

Acknowledgments

I wish to acknowledge an entire team of friends and supporters who helped in the production of this guide. Without their suggestions, knowledge, and guidance the following selections would not be nearly as interesting. In particular, I relied upon Ted and Joan Wilentz, who, in addition to writing a marvelous preface to this book, provided me with delicious lunches and encouraged me along the way with their firsthand information about many of the personages and places cited. For over fifty years, the Wilentz family has been involved with literary life in New York City and their help and friendship is a blessing.

Many welcome ideas and needed facts were also provided by Bob Rosenthal, Peter Hale, Bill Gargan, Gordon Ball, Bill and Vicky Keogan, Sean Wilentz, Robert and Patricia Sutherland-Cohen, David Carter, Jack Hagstrom, and Simon Pettet. Thanks to the publisher for guiding me through the maze; Helene Silver, Melisa Coburn, Daria Masullo and Erica-Cheyenne Moore in particular, and to Peter Simmons, Eileen Morales and Elizabeth Ellis of the Museum of the City of New York for all their work researching the pictures in this book. A special thanks to Tristana Maccio for the stylish illustrations. Always at the center of all this work was my wife, Judy Matz, who deserves all of the credit for keeping me on track.

About the Author

Bill Morgan is a writer, painter, and archival consultant. He received his Masters in Library Science from the University of Pittsburgh and currently lives in New York City. He has worked as an archivist for Allen Ginsberg, Lawrence Ferlinghetti, Gregory Corso, and Lionel Trilling. He is also the author of *The Beat Generation in New York: A Walking Tour of Jack Kerouac's City*.

About the Museum

The Museum of the City of New York is a nonprofit, private educational institution established in 1923 to collect, preserve, and present original materials related to the history of New York City. Most of the photographs in this book are drawn from the museum's vast archives.

Photograph and Illustration Credits and Copyrights

The Museum of the City of New York: 12, 13, 14, 15, 17, 19 (Byron Collection), 23, 27 (1914 photo by Arnold Genthe), 37, 39 (Lucas-Monroe Collection), 42, 43 lower right, 47 (Theater Collection), 50, 51, 56, 58 (Theater Collection), 61 (Byron Collection), 63 (Byron Collection), 84, 86, 89 (top and bottom, Byron Collection), 92 and 93 (monograph of the work of McKim, Mead & White), 95 (Leonard Hassam Bogart Collection), 96 (Theater Collection), 99 (right), 101, 102, 107 (Wurts Collection), 108 (Byron Collection), 112, 118, 134 (Leonard Hassam Bogart Collection), 142 (Leonard Hassam Bogart Collection), 148 (Theater Collection).

Bill Morgan: 16, 21, 24, 26, 28, 29, 30, 33, 35, 43, 52 (courtesy of Ted Wilentz), 59, 64, 70, 73, 80, 90, 100, 126, 129, 133, 136, 139, 140, 145, 146.

© Ginsberg Trust: 44, 65, 69, 71, 79, 82, 143.

Cara Moore: 110, 124

Courtesy of St. Mark's Church: 77

Courtesy of the Algonquin Hotel: 97

Courtesy of the Grolier Club: 115

Courtesy of New York Shakespeare Festival: 121

Courtesy of William Gargan: 144

Literary Portraits by Tristana Maccio: 25, 48, 53, 54, 67, 81, 98, 105, 110, 120, 123, 124, 131, 141, 150.

"These books are filled with shiny objects of information and advice, like the counters of old-fashioned variety stores."

-The *New York Times*

Welcome to
City & Company
Guidebooks
from Universe Publishing

NEW YORK'S 50 BEST PLACES TO FIND PEACE AND QUIET

Allan Ishac

"If you're at wit's end and frantic for tranquility, relax... you can buy a sweet little book..." -The *New York Times*. Now with 10 additional locations. SECOND EDITION

128 pp 0-7893-0834-7 $12.95

NEW YORK'S 50 BEST PLACES TO TAKE CHILDREN

Allan Ishac

Here's a guaranteed good time for kids ages 1–12 and for their parents, grandparents, and teachers, too.
SECOND EDITION

160 pp 0-7893-0836-3 $12.95

CITY WEDDING: A GUIDE TO THE BEST BRIDAL RESOURCES IN NEW YORK, LONG ISLAND, WESTCHESTER, NEW JERSEY, AND CONNECTICUT

Joan Hamburg
Joan Hamburg of WOR's *The Joan Hamburg Show* and the annual WOR Bridal Show provides an all-in-one resource guide to planning a wedding in New York City—from gowns and tiaras to florists and photographers. This completely revised second edition has many new entries. SECOND EDITION

288 pages 0-7893-0856-8 $18.95

CITY BABY: THE ULTIMATE GUIDE FOR NEW YORK CITY PARENTS FROM PREGNANCY TO PRESCHOOL

Kelly Ashton and Pamela Weinberg
"Everybody should have a book like this." —Carol Jenkins, Fox News
Learn how to take care of yourself (prenatal yoga classes, childbirth methods, birthing centers) and your baby (pediatricians, au pairs, Mommy & Me programs) with this indispensable guide to the best resources, shops, and programs New York City has to offer.
SECOND EDITION

288 pages 0-7893-0832-0 $18.95

THE COOL PARENTS' GUIDE TO ALL OF NEW YORK

Alfred Gingold and Helen Rogan
Cool parents Gingold and Rogan "offer tantalizing details on stuff you can't find in other guides" said *New York Magazine* and the *New York Times* raved that the activities offered "are chosen as much for the pleasure of the parents as for the children." This completely revised third edition has many new entries. Great for out-of-towners!
THIRD EDITION

144 pp 0-7893-0857-6 $14.95